Using Personal Computer Software Workbook

to accompany

STERN • STERN

An Introduction to Computers and Information Processing

SECOND EDITION

Prepared by
Robert A. Stern
Nancy Stern
Edward C. Hackleman

JOHN WILEY & SONS • NEW YORK CHICHESTER BRISBANE TORONTO SINGAPORE

ISBN 0 471 82667 7 - not for sale; and
ISBN 0 471 82993 5 - for sale

Printed in the United States of America

10 9 8 7 6 5 4 3 2 1

PREFACE

This workbook accompanies <u>An Introduction to Computers</u> <u>and Information Processing</u>, 2nd edition, by Robert A. Stern and Nancy Stern. It can be used as a stand-alone guide to personal computers (PCs) or as a supplement to the text. It is recommended that you read Chapter 9 in the text before reading Chapters 1-4 in the workbook and that you read Chapter 12 in the text before reading Chapter 5 in the workbook. Chapter 9 in the text focuses on an introduction to micros and Chapter 12 considers BASIC programming.

The workbook has been organized as follows:

Chapter 1   Communicating with your PC

The chapter focuses on commands you need to know to get your PC to operate. The focus is on procedures for using your PC effectively. These include formatting diskettes, making copies of software packages, listing directories, etc.

Chapter 2   An Introduction to Word Processing

PCs are widely used for printing reports, an application with which most readers are apt to be familiar. For this reason, we chose word processing as our first software package. With a brief exposure to word processing, readers will almost immediately realize some of the major benefits of personal computers. The chapter also focuses on how to read menus supplied by a software package. WordStar is the software package considered.

Chapter 3   Data Base Management Systems

Business students are apt to be somewhat familiar with files and file processing. Hence we chose data base management systems as our next application topic. This chapter also considers record layouts, file design, etc. DBase II is the software package considered.

Chapter 4   Electronic Spreadsheets

We saved this popular application package for last because we believe it will have its greatest impact <u>after</u> readers have already become familiar with PCs themselves and some menu and command structures. We believe spreadsheet packages could have the greatest impact on business and hence should, if possible, be tackled <u>after</u> one has an introductory exposure to PCs.

Preface

Since there is no standard or even _de facto_ standard in spreadsheets, we begin by discussing how electronic spreadsheets, in general, function. These concepts are similar for all spreadsheets. We then illustrate these concepts using VisiCalc, SuperCalc, and Lotus 1-2-3, with a brief introduction to Symphony. We include VisiCalc because it has been popular for many years and is apt to be relatively easy for first-time users. We also consider SuperCalc, Lotus 1-2-3, and Symphony which are some of the other, very popular spreadsheet packages.

Chapter 5 Programming in BASICA

This chapter considers the special features common to BASICA which is a PC version of BASIC. Since BASIC _programming_ concepts are provided in the main text in Chapter 12 and Appendix A, this chapter in the workbook focuses on BASICA syntax, general file processing using BASICA, and an introduction to graphics and sound in BASICA.

Each chapter includes some practice problems to help in getting started as well as a self-evaluating quiz, with solutions.

The material in this workbook is meant as a basic introduction to the five topics outlined above. The chapters should help familiarize you with these topics but they do _not_ provide a comprehensive view. Each chapter will be enough to get you started. Once you have mastered this general introduction, you should consult the appropriate user's manual.

The packages described in this workbook have been tested on an IBM PC with a DOS operating system. You may be using a different computer and/or a different operating system. Note that these packages may be run on a wide variety of PCs using other operating systems. You may find, however, that there are minor variations both in instructions and in keyboard use depending on your PC.

Similarly, your system may support a word processing, data base or spreadsheet package not emphasized here. Nonetheless the concepts and commands discussed in this workbook will be relevant because they have their counterpart in other packages. The most generic chapter in this workbook is on spreadsheets where numerous packages are considered.

BASICA, discussed in this workbook, is a version of BASIC for IBM and IBM-compatible PCs. Other micro-based versions of BASIC tend to be very similar.

Trademarks of Material Mentioned in This Workbook

PC-DOS and IBM are registered trademarks of International Business Machines Corporation.

MS-DOS is a registered trademark of Microsoft Corporation.

CP/M is a registered trademark of Digital Research.

SuperCalc is a registered trademark of Sorcim Corp.

dBaseII, dBaseIII, and Framework are registered trademarks of Ashton-Tate.

WordStar, MailMerge, and SpellStar are registered trademarks of MicroPro International.

1-2-3 and Symphony are registered trademarks of Lotus Development.

VisiCalc is a registered trademark of VisiCorp.

CONTENTS

CHAPTER 1

COMMUNICATING WITH YOUR PC

A. OBJECTIVES OF THIS WORKBOOK

Many introductory computer courses focus on using microcomputers, commonly referred to as personal computers or PCs. Instructors of such courses frequently ask students to learn the basics of a PC and to be able to use, in a very fundamental way, common software packages for typical business applications.

The purpose of this workbook is to provide you with enough basic information to be able to turn on a PC, to call in sample packages, and to actually get these packages to run. We provide a step-by-step, simplified workbook approach to first-time users. This guide is intended only to get you started. If more detail is desired, you will need to consult a user's manual. Since many manuals are difficult for first-time users to understand, this introduction will help to teach you the basics before you read the manual.

You should read Chapter 9 of An Introduction to Computers and Information Processing, 2nd edition first to familiarize you with the features of PCs.

Now, welcome to the world of the PC. We believe you will find this world both exciting and challenging!

B. GETTING STARTED

1. What You Need to Get Started

As you are aware there are numerous types of personal computers (PCs) available. They are all fairly similar in appearance and can, in general, perform similar functions. We will consider typical components of a PC and provide illustrations of how operations are performed; we use the IBM or IBM-compatible PC to highlight these examples. If your PC fits into the category of IBM-compatibles, no additional sources will be needed to get started. If not, read the topics discussed and either ask someone or consult a user's manual if your computer differs from what is described.

We will assume your computer comes equipped with the following input/output devices:

1. Keyboard

2. Monitor

3. At least one disk drive

4. A printer

We will also assume you have some software packages available to you. You will need the following:

Chapter	Package
1	DOS
2	WordStar (or comparable word processing package)
3	dBase II or dBase III or Framework
4	VisiCalc, SuperCalc, 1-2-3, or Symphony
5	BASICA

The version of the software package, typically specified as 1.0, 2.1, etc., does not matter for now, since we will be focusing only on the basics.

2. Interpreting the Keyboard

Keyboards are not always identical, but most keyboards include similar characters. We will focus on the IBM-PC keyboard as illustrated in Figure 1.1. If your keyboard is different, most of the following elements will apply anyway; you may need to experiment or check your manual to learn about some special features available on your computer's keyboard.

We provide a brief introduction to some of the more important keys on the keyboard.

a. The Keys Used for Data Entry

The basic keyboard on most PCs resemble keys on a typewriter. The carriage return key on your PC may be designated as ⏎, ENTER or RETURN. See Figure 1.1 again for an illustration of the carriage return key, designated as ◄──┘ .

You type commands and data using your keyboard as if it were a typewriter. When you are ready to send a line to the CPU, hit the ◄──┘ or RETURN key. No data or command is transmitted until this key is depressed. Thus, you can make changes to a command before transmitting it.

If a mistake is made as you are keying, use the backspace key to backspace and erase characters. Each time you press the backspace key, the computer will delete one character at the cursor point.

In addition to the ◄──┘ or RETURN key there are other keys that may not be familiar to you. Figure 1.2 provides an overview of the purpose of some of these special keys that appear on the keyboard.

b. Numeric Keypad

The numeric keypad is typically located to the right of the main keyboard. See Figure 1.1 again. The numeric keypad allows you to enter numbers conveniently. It may be used in place of the numbers on the top row of the main keyboard. Frequently, control characters appear below the numbers on a numeric keyboard, as on an IBM or IBM-compatible computer. On such devices, you must depress NUMLOCK once to ensure that the numeric keypad will transmit the numbers and not control characters. In this sense, NUMLOCK works like a shift key. To be able to enter control characters after numbers have been transmitted, press the NUMLOCK key once again. It is sometimes more handy to use the numeric keypad since your right hand can then be used for entering a series of digits.

c. Cursor Arrows

Cursor arrows typically appear on the numeric keypad. These are for cursor control. By depressing cursor control characters, you can reach any point on the screen. That is, you can move to different lines of a display; you may also use the arrows to move to the right or left of a line to make changes as needed. Most packages use cursor keys for designating specific commands or correcting data.

d. Function Keys

Many operating systems and programs make use of function keys for repeating a line entered, selecting items from a menu, etc. That is, a specific function key may automatically result in a task such as repeating a line, without the need to actually retype a command. On IBM PCs these function keys appear to the left of the main keyboard. See Figure 1.1. That is, a specific function key may automatically result in a task such as repeating a line, without the need to actually retype a command. Function keys are typically numbered F1-F10. The meaning of these keys varies significantly from one system to another and will, therefore, not be discussed in detail. Function keys are best used in conjunction with specific programming languages and software packages. As we will see, they have specific meaning for each package.

3. The Monitor

When you type a message to the computer, or when the computer responds to you, the data is displayed on the monitor. Another name for a monitor is cathode ray tube (CRT) or video display. Some monitors have a special "on" switch separate from the computer's "on" switch. If there is a switch or knob on the monitor marked "on/off," turn it on before getting started.

Monitors usually come with a knob for adjusting the screen's color. Feel free to make adjustments as necessary.

4. The Printer

Printers are used to obtain a written copy of disk files or data displayed on the screen. Sometimes specific commands are necessary to enable the printer to work properly. More on this later.

C. USING AN OPERATING SYSTEM

An operating system is a collection of programs that supervises the overall operations of a computer and aids in the effective use of the computer's resources. See Chapter 13 in the text for a full discussion of operating systems.

You must have the operating system in a disk drive before you turn your computer on. Otherwise the computer will not know what to do.

There are numerous operating systems available with PCs. Among the most popular are:

COMMON OPERATING SYSTEMS

Name	Abbreviation for	Characteristics
DOS	Disk Operating System	MS-DOS and PC-DOS are two versions of this disk operating system. These are the most common operating systems for IBM and IBM-compatible PCs.
CP/M	Control Program for Microprocessors	The standard CP/M is widely used on older 8-bit computers; CP/M-86 is common for computers that use an 8086 chip such as the IBM PC.
UNIX		UNIX was originally designed for mainframes; however, it is now available for PCs as well; a common version of UNIX for PCs is called XENIX.

There are many other operating systems but the above three are the most common and account for 90% of all PC applications. The two versions of DOS, MS-DOS and PC-DOS, account for 75% of all PC applications. Thus, we will focus on DOS.

The operating system used with your PC depends on

1) the computer itself: each operating system is designed for specific types of computers;

2) the software packages to be used: each software package can be run with a specific operating system.

A heavy user of the IBM PC, for example, may have numerous operating systems.

You will need to learn some basic commands available with your operating system in order to get started. Note that we include here only an introductory approach to these commands and have made no attempt to be comprehensive. To do so would be beyond the scope of this workbook. You are

provided with enough data to get started with your operating
system and to use it for the software discussed in the
subsequent chapters.

All operating systems provide similar options. You may
find, however, that the command structure differs slightly
from one operating system to another. As noted, we will focus
primarily on DOS commands.

D. THE MECHANICS OF ACCESSING THE COMPUTER

1. Turning Your Computer On

Each PC comes equipped or "configured" with certain
hardware. As noted, you will probably have a keyboard,
monitor or screen, and one or more disk drive(s); you may
also have a printer and/or other equipment. If you have a
floppy disk set-up (most systems are configured with these),
you will typically have one or two drives. If you have two,
the one on the left (or the top, depending on the system) is
the main one. It is commonly referred to as the "A" drive.
You may also have a hard disk instead of, or in addition to,
your disk drives.

To get started, you must turn your PC on. The "on"
switch is typically at the back of your PC or on the side.
Finding it may be a chore itself - but once it is found, you
are on your way!

Before actually turning on the PC, you should have a
diskette which contains the operating system in the main
drive. This is typically the "A" drive. This diskette is
needed to control the computer's functions. The operating
system contains the set of control programs that supervise
the computer. As noted, common operating systems are called
"DOS" and "CP/M." Your operating system, then, should be in
the "A" drive before the switch is turned on.[1]

The following notes will help in getting started:

GETTING STARTED

1. If you have floppy disk drives, place the diskette with
   the operating system on it in the A drive.

---

[1]If you are using a hard disk, the operating system should
already be available from the hard disk when you turn your
computer on.

2. Turn the computer on.

3. The red light on the A drive will go on indicating that the disk drive is operating. Note: Do not remove or replace a diskette in a drive when the light is on.

4. Most operating systems automatically perform a computer self-test to ensure that the hardware components are working properly.

5. If there is a problem, you will be advised. If everything is OK, the computer will transmit a message and you will be given a prompt which is a request for a user response. For example, the following messages and prompts appear using the DOS and CP/M operating systems:

   DOS

   Current date is Tue 1-01-1980

   Enter new date: []

                    prompt

   CP/M

   A > []

             prompt

   Note that we will illustrate the prompt with a [].

6. Most operating systems treat upper and lower case letters in the same manner. This means that if you enter a command such as DISKCOPY or Diskcopy or even DiSkCoPy your computer will assume these to be the same.

Starting up a computer system is frequently referred to as "booting" a system. With a diskette containing an operating system on it, you are ready to "boot."

2. Date and Time Routines for DOS

a. Date

With DOS, as noted above, the computer will ask you to "Enter new date." The form of the date entry is mm-dd-yy, where mm is a two-digit month, dd is a two-digit day, and yy is a two-digit year (e.g., 86 for 1986). If you do not want to respond to this request for a date, simply hit RETURN.

b. Time

You may enter the time as hh: mm: ss.xx

hh = Hours

mm = Minutes

ss = Seconds

xx = Hundredths of seconds

Use a colon (:) between hours and minutes and between minutes and seconds. Use a period (.) between seconds and hundredths of seconds.

DOS assumes a 24-hour clock. Thus 1 AM to noon is 01 to 12 respectively; 1 PM becomes 13, 2 PM is 14, etc.

You can enter 1:06 PM, for example as

Enter new time: 13:06:00.00

or simply as:

Enter new time: 13:06

You can ignore the request for both date and time by hitting the RETURN key when "Enter new date:" and "Enter new time:" is displayed. It is, however, useful to make these entries because the date and time will be recorded for each file you create or change. In this way, your directory of files will include the date and time each file was created or changed. The date and time can be a handy reference guide for you. They can also help distinguish between copies of files that you may have created earlier and are now obsolete.

Remember to hit the RETURN key after date and time have been entered.

PRACTICE ASSIGNMENTS

1. Find the "on" switch for your PC (and your monitor, if there is one).

2. Place an operating system diskette in the A drive.

3. "Boot" or start up your system.

4. Respond to any initial prompts.

3. Rebooting

If at any time you need to restart a run, we call this "rebooting." On IBM and IBM-compatible computers, you must press CTRL and ALT and DEL - all together - to reboot. This automatically restarts the system which will then prompt you for a date or for a command.

Other systems may require depressing the CTRL key and the letter C - both at the same time - to reboot. This is frequently designated as ^C where ^ represents the CTRL key.

Note, too, that you can always restart any computer by turning the machine off, waiting 15 seconds or so, and then turning the machine on again, making certain that your operating system diskette is in the "A" drive.

E. COMMON OPERATING SYSTEM COMMANDS

1. Directory (DIR) Command

a. Listing Existing Files

If you type DIR using most operating systems, you will obtain a directory of all files already on your diskette. See Figure 1.3 for an illustration of file names found on one diskette's directory. Note that when you type DIR, you must press the ENTER, RETURN, or ◄─┘ key before the computer responds to the command. Similarly, suppose you type the following instead of DIR:

        A> DER

If you have not yet pressed the ENTER key when you detected the error, hit the backspace key twice. ER will be erased and the letter D will appear as follows:

        A> D

Now key IR and hit the ENTER key. The computer will then respond appropriately.

If you have already hit the ENTER key after typing A>
DER, the computer will tell you that it does not understand
your message by typing "Bad command," or something similar.
Simply reenter your DIR command again and hit the ENTER or
RETURN key.

PRACTICE ASSIGNMENTS

1. Place the operating system in the A drive.

2. Turn the computer on.

3. Respond to the initial prompts.

4. Reboot by depressing CTRL, ALT, and DEL.

5. Type DER and see what happens.

6. Type DIR to obtain a directory.

b. File Names on a Directory

Data and programs are stored on diskettes as _files_. You
will see that each operating system, as well as each software
package, consists of a set of files. To give a command to a
computer, you frequently must tell it to use some existing
files.

You will be accessing files and creating them as well,
as you go along. Each file is defined by a name designated as
a filename and an optional extension as follows:

filename.extension

That is, you define a file with a filename; if you wish to
use an extension as well, it follows the filename. A filename
and its extension are separated by a period. A filename may
contain 1-8 characters consisting of letters, digits, and
most special characters except *, ?, or a space. An extension
also includes letters and digits but can only contain from 1-
3 characters. DISCT.BAS, for example, may be a filename for a
BASIC program (.BAS is an extension) that calculates a DISCT.
Upper and lower case letters are treated as the same
characters in both the filename and the extension.

Extensions used with filenames frequently have specific
meaning to the system. The following are among the more

commonly used extensions with most operating systems:

COMMON EXTENSIONS TO FILENAMES

.COM or .EXE	A filename listed in your directory with an extension of .COM or .EXE is an executable file. By typing the filename (without the extension) the computer will assume you want a command executed.
.BAS	A filename with an extension of .BAS is typically a BASIC program.
.BAK	This is typically a backup of a file.
.DAT or .TXT	This is a data or text file.

As we begin to create files using WordStar, dBase II, and a spreadsheet package, you will become even more familiar with filenames and extensions.

2. Changing Disk Drives

When you begin, the A drive typically provides the prompt. That is, if you type DIR, for example, the computer will assume you want a directory of "A" drive files. To obtain a directory of "B" drive files (if you have a second drive) type:

        A > DIR B:

If the B drive contains a program you want to execute, you may type:

        A > B:

Sometimes you keep your operating system on the A drive and your software package on the B drive. Other times, you place data files on B. If you type B: the computer will respond as follows:

        B >

This means the B drive is now "in charge." An operating system disk should be in the B drive along with any other files and/or programs if you wish to execute a program from the B drive. If it does not, you will need to revert to the A drive again and give the appropriate command. For example, to obtain a directory of files on the B drive, you may type:

        B> A:
        A> DIR B:

On line 1 above, B> is the computer's prompt. You type A: to return control to the A drive. On line 2, A> is again the computer's prompt. You type DIR B: to obtain a listing of files on the B drive.

3. Preparing and Copying Diskettes

Now you know how to start your system, use your keyboard (basically), and obtain a directory of files. Preparing new diskettes so that they can contain copies of files and programs is an important task handled by the operating system. Since diskettes are relatively delicate, you should make duplicate copies of all files just in case a diskette becomes unusable.

Be sure to place a gummed label on each new diskette and then write the name of the programs stored on that diskette. Without this label you would not be able to identify the contents of the diskette. Gummed labels are available in each box of diskettes.

a. Formatting

Formatting tells the computer how data is to be put on a diskette. To format a diskette is similar to indicating whether a report should have single or double spacing. Blank diskettes must be formatted <u>before</u> <u>they</u> <u>can</u> <u>be</u> <u>written</u> <u>on</u>. Thus, a diskette cannot be used for storing or copying files or programs unless it has first been formatted. The following basic FORMAT command specified prior to a COPY command will provide a standard format for your diskette:

        A> FORMAT B:

Be sure to hit the ENTER key when you are done. The computer will format the diskette that is in the B drive. The computer will respond with the following message:

        Insert new diskette for drive B:
        and strike any key when ready []

Hit any key and the computer will respond:

        Formatting ... Format complete

           362496 bytes total disk space

           362496 bytes available on disk

        Format another (Y/N)? []

     To format a diskette in the B drive so that 1) it is
formatted <u>and</u> 2) it contains the DOS operating system as
well, type <u>A></u> FORMAT B:/S.

     Note that the FORMAT command deletes all previous
information stored on the diskette. Thus if the diskette in
drive B already had data on it, the format statement will
erase it. You should therefore be very careful when using the
format statement. Make certain that the diskette does <u>not</u>
contain needed data.

     Once formatted, a diskette can then be used to create
files or to copy existing ones.

PRACTICE ASSIGNMENT

1. Take a blank diskette (or one with unneeded data), place
   it in the B drive, format it, and place the operating
   system on it as well.

b. <u>Copying</u>

     As noted, it is important to create backup copies of
diskettes. A diskette can easily become damaged; moreover,
sometimes you may accidentally delete or erase files. To
minimize the risk of the latter, label all diskettes using
gummed labels provided in the box of diskettes. Use a felt-
tipped pen for writing on the label.

     To copy files from one diskette to a second (formatted)
diskette, use the COPY command. Consider the following:

        COPY A:FILE1.DAT B:

This command copies the file called FILE1.DAT, a data file,
from the A drive to the B drive. At the end of the operation,

FILE1.DAT will appear on both the A and B diskettes. The COPY command is directly followed by the drive where the existing file may be found and the name of the file; this in turn is followed by the drive name which will contain the file to be copied. Omitting the filename after B: means that the second drive will contain a file with the same name.

To copy all files from the A drive to the B drive, type:

        COPY   A:*.*   B:

The computer would respond with a listing of all files copied and a message such as:

        23 file(s) copied

The *.* is a way of saying "all" files.

c. DISKCOPY

DISKCOPY is a simplified command used to both format a new diskette called a target diskette and to copy the entire contents of the source diskette onto it. DISKCOPY then backups an entire diskette.

If your system has two disk drives, you type DISKCOPY A: B: The computer will typically respond with:

        Insert source diskette in drive A:

        Insert target diskette in drive B:

        Strike any key when ready

When copying, the computer will display:

        Copying 9 sectors per track, 1 side(s)

        Copy complete

        Copy another [Y/N]? []

The source diskette is the original, to be copied; the target diskette contains the copy. At end, type N for no more copies.

If your system has only one diskette, type DISKCOPY A: A:

The computer will respond with:

        Insert source diskette in drive A:

Strike any key when ready

Copying 9 sectors per track, 1 side(s)

Insert target diskette in drive A:

Strike any key when ready

Take the source diskette out, place the target diskette in the A drive and then strike any key. The computer will typically type:

Copy complete

Copy another (Y/N)?

Type N when you are done. If, instead of the above, the computer responds by instructing you to place the source diskette into the A drive again, follow the directions. This might be necessary if a diskette contains a great deal of data and all of it cannot be copied at one time.

Note that the message you will receive from the computer may vary slightly depending upon the version of DOS you are using.

In Section H of this chapter, we indicate how important it is to have backup copies of diskettes for protection. To preserve your diskettes and to minimize the risk of losing data, keep diskettes in their paper envelopes, do not touch any part of the diskette except the envelope, and be careful when inserting it in the drive.

d. DISKCOPY vs COPY

Note the following about DISKCOPY as compared to the COPY command:

1. DISKCOPY is not available on all versions of DOS.

2. DISKCOPY does not work well if some sectors of either the source or the target diskette are bad.

3. DISKCOPY is faster than COPY.

4. DISKCOPY erases the contents of the target diskette because it automatically formats the target diskette before writing on it.

5. COPY merges new files from the source diskette with old files on the target diskette.

6. With DISKCOPY, there is no need to format a new diskette.

e. CHKDSK

A CHKDSK command performs the following:

    1) Checks to see how much space is available on the diskette.

    2) Indicates how much space is being used by the diskette.

    The following is a typical response to a CHKDSK command:

        362490 bytes total disk space
         40960 bytes total memory
        321530 bytes free

f. Protecting a Diskette from Being Written On

    Each diskette has a square write protect notch on it. 5 1/4-inch diskettes may be written on if the notch is not covered with a metallic strip or tab. Each package of diskettes comes with write protect tabs that you can use when you want to prevent writing on specific diskettes. Put the tab over the square notch on the diskette and the computer will not write on that particular diskette.

4. Additional DOS Commands: A Capsule View

You Key	Computer Response	When Used
DATE	Current date is XXX-----X Enter new date:	To change the date.
TIME	Current time is X-----X Enter new time:	To change the time.
ERASE filename	None	To delete a file.
REN X--X Y--Y	None	To change the name of a file from X--X to Y--Y.

5. Versions of an Operating System

Operating systems are usually numbered as 1.1, 2.0, and so on. The first digit or integer indicates the major version of the operating system; that is, 1.0 is an older and less advanced version than 2.0, 3.0, etc. If the integer is the same but the decimal component changes (e.g., 1.1, 1.2, etc.), this indicates a minor modification to the same version. Thus DOS 2.1 is a slightly more advanced version than 2.0. Note, however, that changes to integers mean <u>major</u> changes. Thus DOS 3.0 has significant changes over 2.0.

Always obtain the latest version of an operating system. As newer versions become available, users of that operating system can acquire updates for minimal cost. Be sure you obtain the operating system user's manual as well.

This numbering system is also used to represent versions of software packages. Thus WordStar 3.0 is a more up-to-date version than 2.0.

F. AN OVERVIEW OF CP/M COMMANDS

The following CP/M commands are similar to DOS commands:

DOS	CP/M
DIR	DIR
COPY	COPY or PIP
CHKDSK	STAT
ERASE	DEL
FORMAT	FORMAT
REN	REN

Most operating systems perform the same basic commands as above. The precise entry or format may change. There are, of course, many other operations that may be performed. Check your user's manual for additional options.

G. ACTIVATING THE PRINTER

One way to activate the printer is to press the CTRL key at the same time as you press the PrtSc (Print Screen) keys.

When these keys are depressed, DOS will make a printed copy
of whatever is displayed on the screen.

That is, when you press Ctrl and PrtSc together, the
computer will print or echo every line you type. This is one
way of obtaining a written log of your interaction with the
computer. Pressing Ctrl and PrtSc a second time will
deactivate this echo printing.

If you are connecting a printer with an IBM PC you must
typically use the MODE command to provide details about your
printer. See your manual or speak to someone to determine how
the MODE command is used with your printer.

H. PREPARING A WORKING COPY OF A SOFTWARE PACKAGE

a. Make a Copy of an Original Diskette

The original diskette supplied by the manufacturer
should be copied onto a working diskette and then saved. Once
the working diskette is available, put the original in a safe
place. As a general rule, save the original diskette and use
it only to make copies. To ensure that you do not
inadvertently write on the original, cover the write protect
notch with a write protect tab. This tab can be found in the
box in which blank diskettes are supplied.

Most manufacturer-supplied diskettes either allow you to
make a copy from the original or provide you with a copy. If
a diskette is supplied so that it is "copy protected" the
manufacturer will typically provide you with instructions for
preparing a backup. To make a working copy of a diskette, the
target diskette which is the one to contain the copy, must
first be formatted if it is a blank diskette.

b. The Copy Should Contain the Operating System as Well, for Ease of Use

It is also useful for the target diskette to contain a
copy of the operating system if there is room so that you can
"boot" or start up the system with that diskette. If the
package does not contain the operating system you would
always need two diskettes to get started: the diskette that
contains the operating system in the A drive and the one that
contains the package in the B drive.

The simplest way to prepare a working copy, then, is to:

1. Put the operating system (DOS, CP/M, etc.) in the A drive.

2. Retrieve an unused or new diskette. Put a label on it that contains the name of the software package. Each box of diskettes comes with blank labels.

3. Type DISKCOPY A: B: for dual diskette system or DISKCOPY A: A: for single diskette system.

The computer will prompt you for the following:

Source diskette - This is the original diskette

Target diskette - This diskette will contain the copy

Follow the directions that appear on your screen. They will tell you where and when to insert the diskettes. Note that DISKCOPY begins by formatting the target diskette.

After the DISKCOPY is complete the computer will respond with:

COPY another (Y/N)? []

Type N for No.

c. When DISKCOPY is Complete, You Will Have a Target Diskette with the Operating System on it.

You now want to put the package on this target diskette as well. Put the original operating system diskette in the A drive. If you have a dual diskette system, type:

COPY A:*.* B:

If you have a single diskette drive, type:

COPY A:*.* A:

Follow the directions that appear on your screen which tell you where and when to insert diskettes. The source diskette for this second procedure is now the manufacturer-supplied diskette with the software package on it. The target diskette is the same one as previously; that is, it already has the operating system on it. Prepare a label with the name of the package and put it on this diskette.

You use COPY now rather than DISKCOPY because DISKCOPY would begin by reformatting, and reformatting erases the entire diskette. Thus if you had typed DISKCOPY you would erase the operating system from the target diskette.

Figure 1.4 provides a brief summary of the more common DOS commands.

I. LOOKING AHEAD TO THE NEXT CHAPTERS

The remaining chapters focus on specific software packages and on advanced Basic. In each case you are provided with instructions on actually using this software. Before using a new package, you should follow the rules specified in the chapter. If you are already supplied with a copy of a package, rather than the original, you may skip the set of rules in Section H above which focus on obtaining a second copy. Note that these rules are applicable for all packages.

SELF-EVALUATING QUIZ

1. PC is an abbreviation for _____.

2. Another word used to describe PC is _____.

3. The main diskette drive of a PC is typically called the _____ drive.

4. Before turning on a PC, you should have a(n) _____ diskette in the main drive.

5. (T or F) There are usually two sets of keys on a keyboard that can be used for entering numbers.

6. Before data is transmitted to a computer, the _____ key must be depressed.

7. The most common operating system for an IBM PC is called _____.

8. DOS begins by asking the user for a _____.

9. A request from the computer is called a _____.

10. To obtain a listing of all files on your DOS or CP/M diskette type _____.

11. The command DISKCOPY A: B: will result in _____.

12. To determine how much disk space is still available, type _____.

13. To copy an entire diskette onto another, use the _____ command.

14. To copy one or two files from one diskette to another, use the _____ command.

15. (T or F) DISKCOPY automatically formats a disk, but COPY does not.

SOLUTIONS

1. personal computer

2. microcomputer

3. A

4. operating system

5. T - First row of the main keyboard plus the numeric keypad.

6. ENTER or RETURN or ⏎

7. DOS (MS-DOS or PC-DOS)

8. date

9. prompt

10. DIR

11. The contents of the diskette in the A drive being copied onto the diskette in the B drive.

12. CHKDSK (DOS) or STAT (CP/M)

13. DISKCOPY (DOS)

14. COPY

15. T

PRACTICE ASSIGNMENTS

1. Find the "on" switch. Insert an operating system diskette into the A drive.

Turn the system on. Enter today's date and time.

<u>Note</u>: If you have a hard disk follow the directions provided with your system.

2. Obtain a directory of files.

3. Determine how many positions are available on your diskette.

4. Format a blank diskette.

5. Copy DOS onto this new diskette.

6. Determine the differences between

    a. COPY and DISKCOPY

    b. CTRL and ALT and DEL and turning the computer off, then on.

    c. Shift key and Cap Lock.

7. Obtain a printed copy of your directory.

Figure 1.1 IBM PC Keyboard

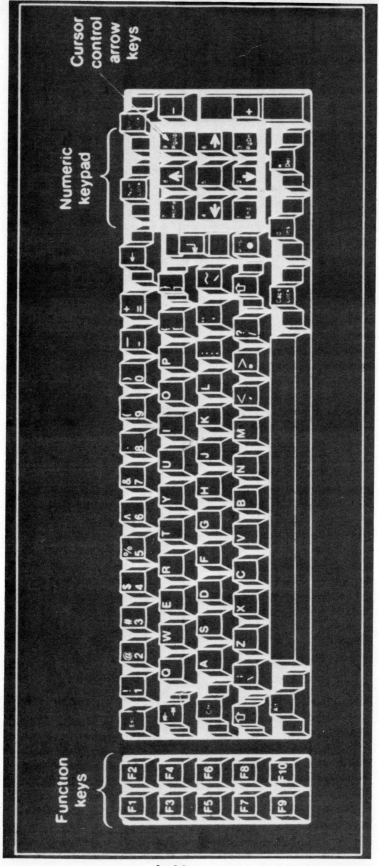

Figure 1.2 Keys to Remember

KEY	Meaning	Use
	ENTER or RETURN Key	Press this key to transmit an entry to the CPU.
	Backspace Key	Use this key to correct errors on a line before the ENTER key has been pressed.
Ctrl Alt Del (separate keys-depress them together)	"Boot" or Start Up	Use to reset or restart the system; same as turning the computer off, then on again; you must have a DOS diskette in the A drive.
Esc	Escape Key	Causes the computer to ignore the current line.
	Tab Key	Moves cursor 8 characters ahead; works like a tab key on typewriter.
	Shift Key	Acts like a shift key; depress once with any character to transmit upper case letters and special characters in place of numbers.
Cap	Cap Lock	Use to obtain upper case letters. When depressed, all letters are upper case. When depressed again returns to lower case.
Ctrl PrtSc	Print Screen	Use to print whatever appears on the monitor.
Ctrl Numlock	Stop the Display	Halts a display so you can read it before it goes off the screen; depress these keys together. Depress the RETURN key to continue the display.

Figure 1.3 Log—On Messages

```
Current date is Tue  1-01-1985
Enter new date:  6-19-86        mo-day-yr
Current time is  0:00:15.21
Enter new time: 1:33:45.1       hr:minute:second:tenths
                                of second


The IBM Personal Computer DOS
Version 2.10 (C)Copyright IBM Corp 1981, 1982, 1983
```

A > DIR

```
COMMAND      COM    4959   5-07-87   12:00P
FORMAT       COM    3816   5-07-87   12:00P
CHKDSK       COM    1720   5-07-87   12:00P
SYS          COM     605   5-07-87   12:00P
DISKCOPY     COM    2008   5-07-87   12:00P
```

↑	↑	↑	↑	↑
filename	file name extension	bytes of disk space used	date created or changed	time created or changed

Using Personal Computer Software Workbook

Figure 1.4   Disk Operating System (DOS) Commands

DIR   Lists a directory of all files on a diskette. Directory
           includes: filename.ext, size in bytes, and date/time
           stamp.

TYPE   Displays the contents of a file on the monitor screen.

ERASE   Erases a file from the diskette.

COPY   Produces a copy of a file.

RENAME   Renames a file.

A: or B: Changes the current drive (the default disk drive
           specification)

ACTION DESIRED   COMMAND SYNTAX

DIR   Current drive is A: Current drive is B:
Directory of A: A>DIR   B>DIR A:
Directory of B: A>DIR B: B>DIR

- -

TYPE
Display a file on A: A>TYPE filename.ext   B>TYPE A:filename.ext
Display a file on B: A>TYPE B: filename.ext B>TYPE filename.ext

- -

ERASE
Erase a file on A: A>ERASEfilename.ext   B>ERASE A:filename.ext
Erase a file on B: A>ERASE B:filename.ext B>ERASE filename.ext

Erase all files with
same ext. on A: A>ERASE *.ext   B>ERASE A:*.ext

Erase all files with
same .ext on B: A>ERASE B:*.ext   B>ERASE *.ext

- -

COPY
Copy a file A: to B: A>COPY filename.ext B: B>COPY A:filename.ext
Copy a file B: to A: A>COPY B:filename.ext B>COPY filename.ext A:

Copy all files with
same .ext from
A: to B: A>COPY *.ext B: B>COPY A:*.ext

CHAPTER 2

WORD PROCESSING USING WORDSTAR

Note: Pages 548-549 of the text provide an introduction to word processing and text editing.

A. GETTING STARTED WITH WORDSTAR

1. Accessing the WordStar Package

There are numerous text editing packages available today, but WordStar by MicroPro International, first developed in 1981, is still one of the most popular. In addition to providing a wide range of word processing capabilities, WordStar may be used in conjunction with other MicroPro products. MailMerge is one such product that can be used to prepare personalized letters. Similarly, SpellStar can check the spelling in a document. Other packages may be used with WordStar as well. Note, however, that WordStar is best known for its text preparation and editing capabilities.

RULES FOR ACCESSING WORDSTAR

1. Be sure you are using a copy of the original package. If not, make a copy as indicated in Chapter 1.

2. Copy your operating system on your WordStar diskette.

3. Place the diskette with the operating system and WordStar in the A drive.

4. Turn the computer on.

5. Enter the date and time as specified (see Chapter 1).

6. When the computer prompts you for a command by displaying A>, type WS:

            A > WS

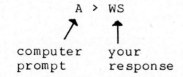

        computer   your
        prompt   response

The letters WS may be typed in either upper or lower case to access the WordStar package. As with most packages, you must hit the ENTER or RETURN key to transmit your message to the computer. The "No File Menu" would then appear on the screen as in Figure 2.1. One of the best features of WordStar is its menu format which makes it relatively easy to learn to use the package.

Remember that there is no need to memorize the various control characters with WordStar. At all times, you may use the menus that appear on the screen to refresh your memory.

2. Editing or Creating a Document

A document is a file created by the WordStar package. Typing a D for document prepares WordStar for document preparation. You type a D, then, to create a new document or to edit an existing one. The computer will respond with:

```
  d    editing no file
       .
       .
       .
       NAME OF FILE TO EDIT?  [] ◄─────── cursor

  DIRECTORY of disk A:
       .
       .
       .
```

After the message "editing no file" appears, some rules about file names follow - we will discuss these later. Then WordStar prompts you for the actual file name by typing:

NAME OF FILE TO EDIT?

The cursor [] is set at this line prompting you for the name of the file you wish to edit or create. You should respond with either 1) an existing file name from the directory, if you wish to modify a file that has already been entered, or 2) a new file name if you wish to create a new file.

Note that a file can be any type of document - a letter, report, chapter, etc. Rules for forming new file names appear right on the screen along with the "editing no file" menu. See Figure 2.2. Note that the rules for forming file names are similar for most software packages.

B. ARRIVING AT WORDSTAR'S MAIN MENU

If you entered a file name that is already in the directory, then the file exists and the computer assumes you want to edit it. The text will be called in, and will appear on the screen. If the screen cannot display the entire text because it is too long, then only the first segment will appear. This segment directly follows the main menu; that is, it occupies the bottom half of the screen. Note that the menu is separated from the text by a dashed line. See Figure 2.3 for an illustration of an existing text which appears along with WordStar's main menu.

If you entered a new file name that was not in the current directory, the main menu would appear as in Figure 2.4 but the lower half of the screen would be blank. The cursor would point to the first line after the main menu, indicating that the computer is ready to accept a new text. To ensure that you are indeed working on a new file, the words "NEW FILE" will flash on the screen followed by the main menu. The file name will also appear at the top of the screen verifying the fact that no previous file with that name exists. Examine the following computer-generated entry which could appear on the top of your screen after you typed WS, for WordStar, and TEST.DOC for the name of a new file:

A: TEST.DOC PAGE 1 LINE 1 COL 1

This response from the computer denotes that your new file is called TEST.DOC and that it will be stored on the diskette in the A drive. PAGE 1 LINE 1 COL 1 indicates that you are at the beginning of the file.

C. ENTERING A NEW TEXT

Let us assume you have entered a file name that does not appear in₁the directory and that you want to begin keying a new text. You may begin typing your text at this point as if you were using a typewriter. Note the following advantages of WordStar which are features not always available when using a typewriter:

1
 If you inadvertently entered a file name that already exists, type ^KQ to abandon this file; then, type your new file name.

1. You need not hit carriage return at the end of a line; that is, WordStar will automatically include margins at the end of a line and proceed to the next line.

2. You need to hit carriage return (ENTER, RETURN or ⬅⏎) only when you wish to end a paragraph.

3. The Tab key may be used for indenting the first letter of a paragraph.

4. The DEL (delete) or backspace key may be used for deleting individual characters to the left of the cursor.

5. WordStar automatically single spaces and allows for 66 characters per line. To double space, key ^OS 2; to triple space key ^OS 3; etc. ^ is used to denote the control key usually labeled on most PCs as CTRL. To type ^OS, hit the control key and hold it down as you hit the letter O and then the letter S; then type 2 for double spacing, etc.

6. Once the file you wish to create has been entered, you may save or store it by typing ^KS.

7. To print the file after you have saved it by typing ^KS, type P and respond to the questions on the screen. The computer will ask you where in the file to start printing, how many copies you want, etc. (You may simply hit the ESC (escape) key to start at the beginning of a file and to obtain a single copy.) Be sure the printer is turned on before you hit ESC.

If you are prepared to edit each line as you are typing it, then the above seven steps is all that is necessary to use WordStar. If you make a mistake on a line simply backspace or hit the DEL key until you have reached the error point and have erased the error; then proceed. Note that there are many other options available with WordStar but the above list will enable you to get started and to type a document.

PRACTICE ASSIGNMENT

Familiarize yourself with WordStar by entering the 17-line text that appears in Figure 2.3. Use the above 7 rules to enter the text. Hit ^KS to save the file and P to print it.

D. EDITING AN EXISTING TEXT

The above rules will familiarize you with entering a new text using WordStar. If, however, you wish to scan the text just entered before printing it, or change an existing text, add to it, etc., you will need to use some of WordStar's special features. Editing a text is frequently referred to as text editing and can be performed with the help of the Main Menu. The Main Menu points to various options available to the user. Remember that to reach the Main Menu, type:

1. D for document file.

2. File name - use a name that already appears in the directory to edit an existing file.

1. Using the Main Menu to Edit an Existing Text

The Main Menu is subdivided into four sections:

```
       1                    2              3                4
                        |            |                |
--Cursor Movement---    | -Delete-   | -Miscellaneous- | -Other Menus-
                        |            |                |
```

See Figure 2.4 which illustrates WordStar's main menu.

The instructions outlined under "Cursor Movement" in the leftmost quadrant (or quarter) of the screen shows you how to skip or move the cursor to different parts of an existing text. The ^ character is an abbreviation for the control key, typically labeled CTRL on most keyboards. ^S, for example, means depress the control key and the S key together.

The main menu states: "^S char left" in the first quadrant labeled 1. This means that each time you depress the control and S keys together, the cursor will move one character to the left. Similarly, as noted in the main menu, each time you hit ^A, the cursor will move one word to the left. ^E brings the cursor to the previous line and ^X brings it to the following line. ^D moves the cursor one character to the right and ^F moves it one word to the right.

These cursor control keys will enable you to reach specific points in an existing text so that you can make changes to it. These keys can locate various items in a text that need to be changed. Once an error is found, new entries may be keyed and old ones deleted as necessary. You may also skip to different pages more easily by keying ^C to move up a

page and ^R to move down a page. This is referred to as
scrolling.

   To ensure that paragraphs are aligned properly after
changes are made, hit ^B. This reformats an entire paragraph
from the cursor point to the end of the paragraph. Sometimes
the computer will respond by asking you whether you wish to
hyphenate a word; just hit RETURN if you wish to ignore the
request. Or, you may request specific hyphenation as
indicated in the main menu.

PRACTICE ASSIGNMENTS

Retrieve the file you entered by typing D and the file name.
If you have forgotten the file name you chose, check the
directory.

1. If you have entered the text in Figure 2.3 make the
   following changes:

   line 1   Omit "As indicated previously,"
                 Begin paragraph with: "There are no ...

   line 2   Change "In this book" to "Here"

   line 4   Change "4K" to "16K"

   line 4   Change "under $100" to "several hundred
                 dollars"

2. Reread your text and make any corrections necessary.

3. Save the new text by keying ^KS; then print it by keying
   P. The P command will prompt you for a file name. Your
   newly saved file has replaced the previous one. After you
   enter the file name, the print command will prompt you for
   options. For simple printing, just hit RETURN as a
   response to each prompt. The computer will print one copy
   of your file.

      If you had wished to keep an old copy of a file as
   well as the new one, you must copy the old into a
   different file before working on it. Use O for copy as
   indicated in the main menu.

2. Deleting Characters Using the Main Menu

In summary, the leftmost quadrant or quarter of the MAIN MENU indicates how to control cursor movement to access specific lines on a screen. As noted, moving to a different line of a text is called scrolling. You need to control cursor movement in order to perform most types of text editing.

The second quarter of the MAIN MENU indicates how characters being keyed can be deleted. ^G deletes a character at the cursor point. The DEL or delete key eliminates the character to the left of the cursor, that is, the previous character keyed. Access your existing text once again and test these keys.

^T deletes the word following the cursor and is used frequently for editing an existing text. ^Y eliminates an entire line at the cursor point. Be careful when using these delete keys. Once an entry has been deleted, it cannot be retrieved again; thus, if you accidentally delete something, you must re-key it.

3. Miscellaneous Text Editing Using the Main Menu

All straightforward editing can be performed with the above control characters that control cursor movement and character deletion.

The items in the third quarter of the MAIN MENU labeled Miscellaneous have the following meaning:

Control Character	Label	Meaning
^I	Tab	Each time ^I is keyed, the cursor moves five positions to the right. This is similar to hitting the Tab key on a typewriter.
^B	Reform	A text entered using WordStar is automatically formatted into paragraph form. Once you make changes to an existing paragraph, however, you must reformat to ensure that the edited or changed text is also in paragraph form. ^B is used to reform a paragraph that has been modified.

Control Character	Label	Meaning
^V	INSERT ON/OFF	When WordStar is first "booted" or called into the computer, INSERT ON will typically appear at the upper right section of the screen. This means that during editing, depressing a character at the cursor point will cause this character to be <u>inserted</u> at the cursor point. If you hit ^V, the INSERT OFF option will appear on the screen. If INSERT OFF is used, then depressing a character at the cursor results in character replacement. That is, the character already at the cursor point will be <u>replaced</u> by the new character. Thus characters are substituted for others, not added to them, if INSERT OFF appears. To revert back to the INSERT ON mode for inserting additional characters, hit ^V before making any insertions.
^L	Find/Replace again	This is identified as "Find/Replace again." It enables you to locate given words or phrases in an existing text. It also enables you to replace one word or phrase with another. The computer will prompt you for the entry to find in the existing text. It will also prompt you for the entry to serve as a replacement. When the entry to be found is located, your response to the "replace" prompt will be substituted.
RETURN	End paragraph	Whenever you hit RETURN, the computer will assume you have reached the end of a paragraph. An end of paragraph arrow, <, will appear at the end of the text line indicating that the paragraph has been completed. The cursor will then point to the next line. To "undo" an end of paragraph arrow (<), use the cursor movement keys to get to the end of a line. Then delete the "<" by depressing the DEL or ^G key.

Control Character	Label	Meaning
^N	Insert a Return	When editing you may wish to break a paragraph into two or more separate paragraphs. Find the entry to serve as the end of the paragraph. When the cursor is at the space to the right of the last period to be in the paragraph, then hit ^N. The paragraph will end at the cursor point. The rest of the data will appear on the screen as a new paragraph. To indent the first word of this next paragraph, hit ^I, for Tab, then ^B to reformat the entire paragraph.
^U	Stop a Command	^U enables you to "break," or end any command. The computer will respond by asking you if you want to permanently end the command, continue, etc.

PRACTICE ASSIGNMENTS

We assume you have entered the text that appears in Figure 2.3.

1. Change 8K to 8000, 128K to 128,000 in the text.

2. Reformat the entire paragraph.

3. Use ^L to find each occurrence of the word microcomputer and change it to micro.

4. A Review of Submenu Items

The rightmost quarter of the main menu indicates the control characters to use to reach any one of a number of WordStar submenus.

Control Character	Label	Figure Illustrating Menu	Meaning
^J	Help	Figure 2.5	Provides additional

Control Character	Label	Figure Illustrating Menu	Meaning
			instructions for new users.
^K	Block	Figure 2.6	Block commands enable you to copy sections of a file, rearrange sections, write sections on other files, save files, etc.
^Q	Quick	Figure 2.7	Quick commands enable you to flip to other portions of a text quickly. You can skip to the beginning of a text, the end of a text, etc.
^P	Print	Figure 2.8	This command provides instructions for controlling special print options such as underlining, printing characters in boldface, etc.
^O	Onscreen	Figure 2.9	This command provides instructions for formatting data. Double spacing, margins, etc. are controlled using this command.

Thus to obtain any of the above submenus which are relatively self-explanatory, hit ^J, ^K, ^Q, ^P, or ^O. Submenus will appear then on the screen. The best way to familiarize yourself with these submenus is to practice using them.

PRACTICE ASSIGNMENTS

Once again retrieve the text illustrated in Figure 2.3 which has been modified.

1. Underline the word micro in your text.

2. Change the text so that it is triple spaced.

3. Use the Block command to delineate the first sentence – ^KB starts it, ^KK ends it. Then write this block (using ^KW) onto a new file. ^KH in your present file will delete all references to the blocking function. When you are done

retrieve the new file you have just created and see if it contains the sentence desired.

Thus WordStar operates with menus in a hierarchical manner. See Figure 2.10 for an illustration of how submenus function using WordStar.

E. ITEMS TO REMEMBER FOR ENTERING A NEW TEXT OR REVISING AN EXISTING ONE

1. Type D for a document file.

2. Enter a file name according to the rules specified on the screen's menu.

3. Be sure the file name does not already appear in the directory if you are entering a new text; if it does, hit ^KQ to abandon the existing file, then D, then the new file name.

4. Enter your text.

5. Useful keys for formatting:

   ^I   Tabs or indents for a new paragraph

   RETURN   Hit RETURN to end a paragraph. To continue with the same paragraph, just keep keying; the computer will automatically format the paragraph as you are keying.

   DEL   Each time you hit the DEL key, one character to the left of the cursor will be deleted.

   ^G   Use to delete one character at the cursor point.

   ^OS n   Use ^OS to change from single spacing to another type of spacing. ^OS 2, for example, causes double spacing.

   ^OL n   Use ^OL or ^OR to change left and right
   and   margins. Hit ^OL or ^OR and the number of
   ^OR n   characters to appear either as the left or the right margin.

You should now be able to enter a text and make changes

to it. Figure 2.11 provides a quick reference to basic
WordStar commands.

Note that the rules above apply to the WordStar word
processing package. Most other text editing or word
processing packages provide similar features but these may be
accomplished in different ways. If you become familiar with
WordStar and then use another package, you will find that you
can learn the new rules easier than someone who has no
familiarity with a text editor at all.

SELF-EVALUATING QUIZ

Note: You may wish to consult Figure 2.11 for a quick
reference.

1. To access the WordStar package type _____, then type
   _____.

2. (T or F) A file name may typically be 1 to 8 characters
   with an optional three character extension. These rules
   are similar with most software packages.

3. (T or F) WordStar is said to be a menu driven software
   package.

4. After accessing WordStar, type _____ to indicate
   that you wish to enter a document file.

5. (T or F) To enter a new text, type a file name that
   already appears in the directory.

6. (T or F) When entering a text, you need only hit RETURN
   to end a paragraph; do not hit RETURN at the end of each
   line.

7. To save a file, type _____; to then print the file,
   type _____.

8. To edit an existing text, you would use the _____
   keys to arrive at specific points in the text.

9. To delete characters, type _____.

10. To add characters, type _____.

11. To obtain double spacing, type _____.

12. To go to the end of a text, type _____.

13. To locate a specific word in the text, type _____.

14. (T or F) Help menus, which serve as tutorials, are available using WordStar.

15. (T or F) WordStar has a feature that enables you check spelling.

SOLUTIONS

1. WS; RETURN or ENTER or ⏎

2. T

3. T

4. D

5. F - Enter a file name that is not in the directory.

6. T

7. ^KS (the control key along with K, then S); P

8. cursor control

9. the del key (or ^G)

10. the character at the cursor point (be sure INSERT ON appears on the top righthand corner of the screen; if INSERT OFF appears, type ^V to obtain the INSERT ON option)

11. ^OS 2

12. ^QC

13. ^L - then respond to prompts

14. T - Type ^J for a help menu.

15. T - It is called SpellStar.

PRACTICE ASSIGNMENTS

In each case enter the text, check it for errors, then save and print it.

1. Enter the Preamble to the Constitution.

2. Type your resume.

3. Write a cover letter to accompany a resume that indicates that you are responding to an advertisement for a job.

4. Write a letter to your professor asking for an extension for a paper.

5. Enter the Gettysburg Address.

6. Write a letter to your professor explaining why you missed a quiz.

Figure 2.1   Editing Menu

```
───────────────────────────────────────────────────────────────
        editing no file
            < < < N O - F I L E   M E N U  > > >

  ---Preliminary Commands---  |--File Commands--| -System Commands-
L  Change logged disk drive   |                 |R  Run a program
F  File directory      off (ON)|P  Print a file  |X  EXIT to system
H  SET help level             |                 |
 --- Commands to open a file--|E  RENAME a file |-WordStar Options-
   D  Open a document file     |O  COPY    a file| M  Run MailMerge
   N  Open a non-document file |Y  DELETE a file | S  Run SpellStar

DIRECTORY of disk A:
 CHAPTER.003    CHAPTER.004    CHAPTER.005    CHAPTER.BAK    CHKDSK.COM
 WS.COM         WSMSGS.OVR     WSOVLY1.OVR
───────────────────────────────────────────────────────────────
```

Figure 2.2   Editing: Selecting a File

```
───────────────────────────────────────────────────────────────

  d              editing no file

  Use this command to create a new document file,
  or to initiate alteration of an existing document file.

     A file name is 1-8 letters/digits, a period,
     and an optional 0-3 character type.
     File name may be preceded by disk drive letter A-D
     and colon, otherwise current logged disk is used.

 ^S=delete character     ^Y=delete entry      ^F=File directory
 ^D=restore character    ^R=Restore entry     ^U=cancel command

   NAME OF FILE TO EDIT?

 DIRECTORY of disk A:
   CHAPTER.003    CHAPTER.004    CHAPTER.005    CHAPTER.BAK
   CHKDSK.COM     WS.COM         WSMSGS.OVR     WSOVLY1.OVR
───────────────────────────────────────────────────────────────
```

Figure 2.3

```
     A:CHAPTER.004  PAGE 1  LINE 01  COL 01      INSERT ON
                  < < <    M A I N   M E N U    > > >
    --Cursor Movement--      -Delete-    -Miscellaneous-      -Other  Menus-
^S charleft^D char right |^G char   |  ^I Tab ^B Reform  |(from Main only)
^A word left ^F word right|DEL chr lf|  ^V INSERT ON/OFF  |^J Help  ^K Block
^E line up   ^X line down |^T word rt|^L Find/Replace again|^Q Quick ^P Print
      --Scrolling--       |^Y line   |RETURN End paragraph |^O Onscreen
^Z line up   ^W line down |          | ^N Insert a RETURN  |
^C screen up ^R screen down|         | ^U Stop a command   |
L----!----!----!----!----!----!----!----!----!----!--------R
Entering Text
```

A. Definition of a Micro

As indicated previously, there are no standard definitions that can be used to definitively distinguish one type of computer from another. In this book, we will define a **microcomputer** as a device with a basic internal storage capacity from 4K to approximately 128K, and with a basic cost from under $100 to several thousand dollars. Many computers that fit our category of "micro" can have storage capacities in excess of 128K if they include add-on memory boards; similarly, many micros cost more than several thousand dollars if they are purchased with numerous peripheral devices and sophisticated software. In summary, the range indicated here is not definitive, but it will provide a handy guide for determining which machines are typically classified as micros. In general, computers labeled in advertisements as personal computers, home computers, or small business computers are typically micros that sell for under $1000; those micros that cost more than $1000 in their basic configuration are typically designed for professional use in business or education.

Figure 2.4

```
        A:CHAPTER.004   PAGE 1  LINE 01  COL 01     INSERT ON
                    < < <    M A I N   M E N U    > > >
    --Cursor Movement--        -Delete-      -Miscellaneous-      -Other  Menus-
^S char left ^D char right| ^G char  | ^I Tab  ^B Reform    | (from Main only)
^A word left ^F word right |DEL chr lf| ^V INSERT ON/OFF    |^J Help  ^K Block
^E line up    ^X line down  |^T word rt|^L Find/Replace again|^Q Quick ^P Print
    --Scrolling--           |^Y line   |RETURN End paragraph |^O Onscreen
^Z line up    ^W line down  |          | ^N Insert a RETURN  |
^C screen up ^R screen down |          | ^U Stop a command   |
L----!----!----!----!----!----!----!----!----!----!----!--------R
```

Figure 2.5

```
            < < <    H E L P   M E N U    > > >

                             |                  |---Other Menus--
H  Display & set the help level|S Status line    |(from Main only)
B  Paragraph reform (CONTROL-B)|R Ruler line     | ^J Help   ^K Block
F  Flags in right-most column  |M Margins & Tabs | ^Q Quick  ^P Print
D  Dot commands, print commands|P Place markers  | ^O Onscreen
                             |V Moving text    | Space Bar returns
                             |                 | you  to Main Menu
```

Using Personal Computer Software Workbook

Figure 2.6

```
<<<      B L O C K    M E N U     >>>

-Saving Files- |-Block Operations-| -File Operations-  |-Other Menus-
S  Save & Resume| B Begin   K End  |R  Read    P  Print |(from Main only)
D  Save --- done| H Hide / Display |O  Copy    E  Rename|^J Help  ^K Block
X  Save & exit  | C Copy    Y Delete|J  Delete          |^Q Quick ^P Print
Q  Abandon file | V Move    W Write | -Disk Operations- |^O Onscreen
 -Place Markers-| N Column on (OFF)|L  Change logged disk|Space Bar returns
0-9 set/hide 0-9|                  |F  Directory on (OFF)|you to Main Menu
```

Figure 2.7

```
<<<      Q U I C K    M E N U     >>>

  ---Cursor Movement---   | -Delete- | --Miscellaneous-- | -Other Menus-
S left side   D right side |Y  line rt|F Find text in file|(from Main only)
E top scrn    X bottom scrn|DEL lin lf|A Find & Replace   |^J Help  ^K Block
R top file    C end file   |          |L Find Misspelling |^Q Quick ^P Print
B top block   K end block  |          |Q Repeat command or|^O Onscreen
0-9 marker    Z up   W down |         |  key until space  |Sapce Bar returns
P previous    V last Find or Block    |  bar or other key |you to Main Menu
```

Figure 2.8

```
         < < <    P R I N T   M E N U   > > >

      ------Special Effects------- | -Printing Changes- |-Other Menus-
(begin and end) | (one time each) |A Alternate pitch   |(from Mail only)
B Bold  D Double|H  Overprint char |N Standard pitch    |^J Help  ^K Block
 S  Underscore  |O  Non-break space|C Printing pause    |^Q Quick ^P Print
 X  Strikeout   |F  Phantom space  |Y Other ribbon color|^O Onscreen
 V  Subscript   |G  Phantom rubout | --User Patches--   |Space Bar returns
 T  Superscript |RET Overprint line|Q(1) W(2) E(3) R(4) |you to Main Menu
```

Figure 2.9

```
         < < <   O N S C R E E N   M E N U   > > >

 -Margins & Tabs- |  -Line Functions- |  --More Toggles--    |-Other Menus-
L Set left margin |C Center text      |J Justify    off (ON)|from Main only
R Set right margin|S Set line spacing |V Vari-Tabs  off (ON)|^J Help   ^K Block
X Release margins |                   |H Hyph-help  off (ON)|^Q Quick ^P Print
I Set  N Clear tab|   ---Toggles---   |E Soft hyph  off (ON)|^O Onscreen
G Paragraph tab   |W Wrd wrap off (ON)|D Print disp off (ON)|Space Bar returns
F Ruler from line |T Rlr line off (ON)|P Page break off (ON)|you to Main Menu
```

Figure 2.10

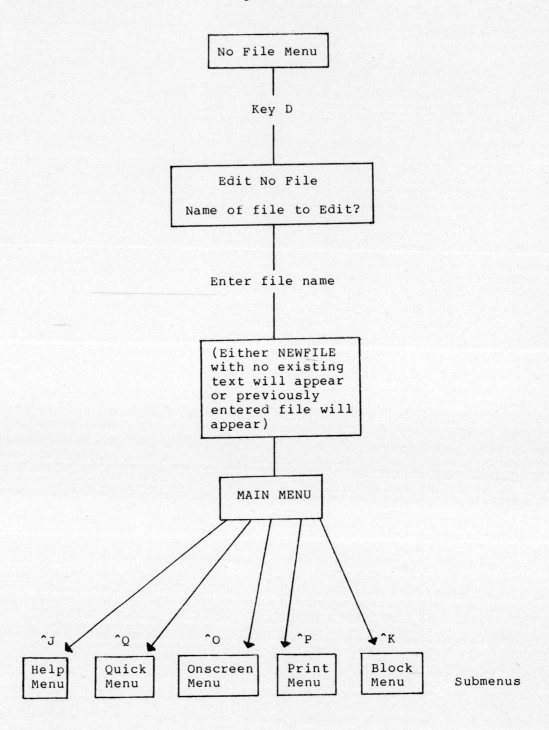

Figure 2.11 WordStar Commands

Quick Reference

Cursor Controls
_____

```
^S    Left character
^D    Right character
^E    Up line
^X    Down line
^A    Left word
^F    Right word
^QS   Left end of line
^QD   Right end of line
Home  Top of Screen
End   Bottom of Screen
^QR   Beginning of file
^QC   End of file
```

Scroll
_____

```
^Z    Scroll down line
PgUp  Scroll down screen
^W    Scroll up line
PgDn  Scroll up screen
```

Delete
_____

```
^Y    Delete line
^T    Delete word right
^G    Delete character right
Del   Delete character left
^Del  Delete to left side of line
^QY   Delete to right side of line
```

Margins
_____

```
^OL   Set left margin
^OC   Center text
^OR   Set right margin
```

Moving Blocks
_____

```
^KB   Mark block beginning
^KK   Mark block end
^KV   Move block
^KC   Copy block
^KY   Delete block
^KW   Write block
^KR   Read block
^KJ   Delete file
^KH   Hide/display markers
```

Print Functions
_____

```
^PB   Triple strike
^PH   Overprint
^PD   Double strike
```

Spacing
_____

```
^OS   Line spacing
```

Miscellaneous
_____

```
^V    Interrupt
^J    Help menu
^JH   Help menu
```

Dot Command Summary
_____

```
.PO   Page offset
.MT   Margin top
.HM   Heading margin
.HE   Heading
.MB   Margin bottom
.FM   Footing margin
```

Special Functions

---

^B   Reform paragraph
^QP   Cursor to previous position
INS   Insert off/on
^OD   Dot command display
^O   Status

Save

---

^KD   Done edit (save the file)
^KS   Save and re-edit
^KX   Save and exit
^KQ   Abandon edit (without saving)

Dot Command Summary

.FO   Footing
.PC   Page number column
.PA   New page
.OP   Omit page numbers
.PN   Page number
.IG   Comment

Note: WordStar is a registered trademark of Micropro International.

CHAPTER 3

DATA BASE MANAGEMENT SYSTEMS USING DBASE II

A. LOOKING BACK: AN HISTORICAL PERSPECTIVE

A decade ago the terms "data base" and "management information system" were frequently used interchangeably. A data base was to contain <u>all</u> data on a company's entire operations. The management information system using this data base was to enable executives to make inquiries about any functional unit within the company. Initial management information systems (MIS) were, however, usually failures because software was not sophisticated enough to handle the magnitude of the task. In addition, executives did not know what questions to ask of the data base to make effective use of the system.

An added problem was that the first data base management systems used existing languages such as COBOL for retrieving data from the data base. Since most end users had no knowledge of COBOL, this made the data base difficult to use. Several years later, query languages were introduced which allowed users to access data but which still needed computer professionals for designing and programming the management information system.

Today there are numerous packages available for micro and mainframe use that enable an end user to develop a data base and to access it as needed. Before considering a specific data base management system for micros, several terms should be clarified.

B. DEFINING A DATA BASE AND A DATA BASE MANAGEMENT SYSTEM

Typically a **data base** contains current information about a company's employees, accounts receivable, accounts payable, inventory, sales, etc. A data base, then, is a collection of interrelated data. A **data base management system** (DBMS) is the set of programs that enable the user to create, update, and retrieve data from a data base.

Using Personal Computer Software Workbook

1. Objectives of a Data Base Management System (DBMS)

A DBMS should have the following goals:

OBJECTIVES OF DBMS

a. To organize data simply and efficiently.

b. To provide timely responses to inquiries.

c. To reduce data redundancy.

d. To reduce cost.

e. To ensure and maintain data security.

f. To permit access by users or noncomputer professionals.

---

2. Functions of a Data Base Management System

A DBMS has many functions. It is typically used to:

1. Create the data base

   A DBMS enables users to define the format of the data in the data base

2. Revise an existing data base

3. Add to an existing data base

4. Edit an existing data base

5. Display portions of the data base

6. Extract specific data from the data base

7. Update the data base

   Add records, change records, modify records

8. Perform calculations on all or some records

9. Prepare reports from the data base

There are now many common data base management systems

designed for micro use. With most of these, the above functions can be performed by a user with little or no previous programming or systems background.

C. DBASE II: AN OVERVIEW

We will focus on a data base management system designed for micros called dBase II and III developed by Ashton-Tate. dBase III, a more advanced version of dBase II, utilizes similar formats as does Ashton-Tate's Framework package.

dBase II may be run on most PCs using either a CP/M or DOS operating system. It is intended for noncomputer professionals as well as experienced programmers. dBase II, unlike packages like WordStar, Lotus 1-2-3, etc. discussed in this workbook, is not specifically menu driven. It is "command driven" which means that the user must consult a manual to learn basic commands and must strictly adhere to the command structure in order to have the system work properly. There are, however, "help" menus designed to serve as tutorials, that is, to explain the various commands. In general, however, a user learns the dBase II commands from a manual.

We will focus on the most common dBase II commands to help get you started.

D. PREPARING FOR A DBASE II PRACTICE SESSION

1. Getting Started

We will use the method of explaining by example to teach the fundamentals of dBase II. The objective is simply to familiarize you with basic dBase II commands used for creating a file, modifying a file, updating a file, and reporting from a file.

Our problem will be to automate the inventory of a small furniture business using dBase II to establish the inventory file. Once the file is created, we will access it in a variety of ways, also using dBase II.

2. Preparing a Backup of Your Diskette

As mentioned previously, all software packages for micros are typically available on diskette. Once you acquire a package on diskette, your first task should be to create a backup copy. The backup copy should include the operating system as well as the software package so that you can "boot" or start up with it directly. If you have not done so already:

a. Put a DOS diskette in the A drive.

b. Copy DOS commands on a fresh "target" diskette by keying:

>   A> DISKCOPY A: B:

Hit the return or enter key to transmit the message.

c. Copy the dBase II diskette onto this same "target" diskette by typing A> COPY A:*.* B:

The computer will ask you to place the target diskette (diskette to be copied) in the B drive. Put the original dBase II "source" diskette into the A drive. The COPY command will copy dBase II onto the B diskette which already has DOS on it.

E. CREATING A DBASE II FILE

1. The CREATE Command

To call in the dBase II package, type dbase after the prompt as follows:

>   A > dbase

Remember to hit return or enter or ◄——┘ in order to transmit a message to the computer. The computer will respond with a . (period). In dBase II, the period means that the system is waiting for a command. No further prompts or menus are given. Thus, you must consult a manual or use a tutorial before accessing dBase II. You may always type "help" to obtain further assistance about system commands in dBase II.

We will begin by creating an inventory file. Since we wish to create a file, we type "create" as a response to the . (period) prompt as follows:

>   .create

The computer then prompts for specific information about the file. Consider the following (the boxed entries are user supplied):

```
A >  dbase
.  create
     ENTER FILENAME:  STOCK
     ENTER RECORD STRUCTURE AS FOLLOWS:
     FIELD       NAME,TYPE,WIDTH,DECIMAL PLACES
     001         COMPANY,C,20
     002         CODE,C,5
     003         ITEM,C,12
     004         DESCRIP,C,10
     005         QTY,N,2
     006         COST,N,7,2
     007         Hit the Return key <CR>
```

Hitting the return key at the end (denoted as <CR>) terminates the record structure format. The boxed entries are user-supplied.

2. Rules for Defining Record Structure

a. Note that all fields within the record are numbered. The first field defined is the first one in the record. Each field will be described by a name, type (character or numeric), width, and number of decimal positions. The NAME of a field must be 10 characters or less. In the above, COMPANY is the first field, CODE the second, and so on.

b. For TYPE, specify C for character or N for numeric. Character fields are those that will contain any combination of characters, letters, digits, etc. N means the field is strictly numeric. Address fields, Name fields and Description fields all would be defined as C. For numeric fields, you should indicate the number of decimal places (after WIDTH). COST, for example, which is the 6th field in the record, is a dollars and cents figure; thus, it has two decimal places, denoted with a 2 under DECIMAL PLACES. If a field is all integers with no decimal places, type 0 under DECIMAL PLACES.

   The filename, called STOCK in our illustration, conforms to rules for forming filenames using most packages: 1 to 8 characters with a 3 character extension, if desired. The extension for dBase II files is frequently specified as .DBF, for "data base file." Our filename STOCK is defined after we type "create".

c. The actual length or WIDTH of any field can be 254 characters. QTY, for example, our fifth field, is defined numerically with 2 integers and no decimal places. ITEM, the third field, is a character field consisting of 12 characters.

F. MODIFYING RECORD STRUCTURES

The above defines a record with 6 fields. To indicate that the RECORD STRUCTURE is complete, we hit the RETURN or ←┘key at the 7th field entry. The computer will respond with:

INPUT DATA NOW?

If we wish to change the format of records before entering data, type:

N

This means "No, we do not wish to enter input data now." If no changes to the record format were necessary and you wished to enter data at this point, you would type Y for yes. We will practice making some changes to the structure before focusing on data entry. Type the following USE command to access the record structure already defined:

. USE STOCK

The USE command calls back into storage the record structure defined for STOCK.

To make changes, type:

. MODIFY STRUCTURE

The MODIFY command provides us with an outline or template of the record. The record format will appear in outline form.

You may use the cursor arrows to arrive at any point on the template. Changes may be made directly to any entry at the cursor point. The following commands, for example, are used to insert or delete a field:

To insert a field: CTRL N (^N)

To delete a field: CTRL T (^T)

To add a field called warehouse, for example:

1. Use the cursor arrows to get to the line after COST

2. Then hit: CTRL N < RETURN >

This enables you to insert a new field. CTRL N is sometimes denoted as ^N.

A blank line is now available for entering a new field.

You can then enter

    WAREHOUSE,C,1

This would be a one position, character field called
WAREHOUSE. To save the amended RECORD STRUCTURE you just
created for the file called STOCK, TYPE:

    CTRL W

CTRL W indicates that you have completed the system command
which in this case was .MODIFY STRUCTURE.

PRACTICE ASSIGNMENTS

1. Access dBase II on your system.

2. Enter the record structure for the file called STOCK as
   described above.

G. RULES FOR ENTERING DATA

To indicate that you wish to enter data, type the following:

    . USE STOCK

    . APPEND

The computer is now ready to accept data. Enter the following
five data records. Each entry can be changed by using the
backspace key before hitting return. To store the entry after
you have checked each line, hit the return key. If you need
to edit a field after it has been entered, use the cursor
arrows to arrive at the point to be changed, make the change
and hit return again.

    The following represents fields of data within STOCK.
The first record has the following fields:

Field Name	Content
COMPANY	AMERICAN DESIGNER
CODE	00197
ITEM	BUREAU

Using Personal Computer Software Workbook

Field Name	Content
DESCRIP	4 DRAWER
QTY	3
COST	219.95
WAREHOUSE	A

Each line then corresponds to a field on the record. We will enter the following 5 data records:

1. AMERICAN DESIGNER
   00197
   BUREAU
   4 DRAWER
   3
   219.95
   A

2. AMERICAN DESIGNER
   00182
   NIGHT STAND
   COLONIAL
   8
   95.00
   A

3. MARYLAND CUSTOM
   00275
   CHAIR
   STUFFED
   2
   129.00
   B

4. MARYLAND CUSTOM
   00279
   SOFA
   STUFFED
   3
   429.00
   B

5. DANISH ADVENTURE
   00060
   WATER BED
   WOOD
   5
   167.00
   B

After the five records have been entered and you are
satisfied that they are correct, hit CTRL W to end the data
entry command. Recall that CTRL W takes you out of the
current command and enables you to enter a new command. The
prompt of a period will appear.

NOTE: You must be consistent in the use of upper and lower
case letters in dBase II. DANISH, for example, is not
considered the same as Danish, with this software package. As
a rule, press CAP LOCK to obtain all capitalized letters and
remain in that mode throughout your dBase II session.

H. RULES FOR DISPLAYING DATA

To display or view the data just entered, use the
DISPLAY command. The following are options that can be used
to see how dBase II displays data:

COMMAND	MEANING
. GO TOP	Goes to the top, that is, the first record (This command is used before specific DISPLAYs to begin at the beginning)
. DISPLAY RECORD 2	Displays the 2nd record
. DISPLAY NEXT 2	Displays the next 2 records (from whatever point you are currently at)
. DISPLAY ALL	Displays all records

Key in the above commands to see if they work properly.

I. RULES FOR RETRIEVING DATA

The DISPLAY command can be used for displaying records
that fit into certain categories. Consider the following
illustrations.

COMMAND	MEANING
. USE STOCK	Accesses the file called STOCK
. DISPLAY ALL FOR WAREHOUSE = "A"	Prints records with a WAREHOUSE of A

COMMAND	MEANING
. DISPLAY ALL FOR COST > 129.00	Prints records with a COST greater than 129.00
. DISPLAY COMPANY FOR WAREHOUSE = "B"	Prints the names of companies using WAREHOUSE B.

PRACTICE ASSIGNMENTS

1. Enter the above five records in the file called STOCK.

2. Change a Code of 00275 to a Code of 00375.

3. Use the DISPLAY verb as above to display:

    a. All records with a warehouse of B.

    b. All records with a cost > 129.00.

    c. Companies using warehouse B.

4. Save the file.

J. PERFORMING CALCULATIONS USING THE REPLACE COMMAND

It is also possible to make changes or to update records in your dBase II file.

Example: To add 8% Sales tax to all cost fields in the five records, type the following:

    . USE STOCK

    . DISPLAY ALL COST

    . REPLACE ALL COST WITH COST * 1.08

    . DISPLAY ALL COST

The REPLACE command, then, is used for changing data.

PRACTICE ASSIGNMENTS

1. Make the above change to the COST figures in your file.

2. Records with a COST figure greater than $100.00 should be given a 2% discount. Make the necessary changes, then display all records.

K. REPORTING FROM A DBASE II FILE

The following options are available to print out a formal report with headings and proper margins. You can display this report on your screen and later, after you have checked it, redirect the output to a printer if hard copy is needed. Boxed entries are user supplied; the rest are prompts from the dBase II package.

```
. USE STOCK
. REPORT
ENTER REPORT FORM NAME: INVENTORY
ENTER OPTIONS, M = LEFT MARGIN, L = LINES/PAGE, W = WIDTH
PAGE HEADING? (Y/N) Y
ENTER PAGE HEADING: INVENTORY REPORT
DOUBLE SPACE: Y
TOTALS: N
SUBTOTALS: N
COL        WIDTH, CONTENTS
001        25,      COMPANY
ENTER HEADING: COMPANY
002        9,      WAREHOUSE
ENTER HEADING: WAREHOUSE
0003       13,      ITEM
ENTER HEADING: DESCRIPTION
return
```

The computer will respond by displaying the report.

To end a dBase II session entirely, type CTRL Q for quit. Recall that you may type CTRL W to terminate a specific command.

You should familiarize yourself with dBase II by typing in the above file called STOCK, displaying records, replacing fields, and writing reports.

Note that the above is only a brief introduction to dBase II. There are many more commands and options available. After you have become familiar with the above, you can look at a dBase II manual or reference guide to learn about the other options available.

Figure 3.1 illustrates important dBase II control keys. Figure 3.2 provides a quick reference guide to the most important commands in dBase II.

SELF-EVALUATING QUIZ

1. (T or F) Initial MIS efforts which attempted to establish data bases were often failures because software was not sophisticated enough to handle the task.

2. (T or F) Today there are numerous DBMS packages available for micro use.

3. (T or F) A user who enters or retrieves data from a DBMS must be familiar with COBOL.

4. (T or F) DBase II can typically be run on most PCs using either a CP/M or DOS operating system.

5. DBase II is said to be _____-driven rather than menu-driven.

6. (T or F) Help menus are available as tutorials with dBase II.

7. To establish a new file using dBase II, type _____.

8. (T or F) Upper and lower case letters can generally be used interchangeably using dBase II.

9. A field name must be (no.) characters or less, but the actual size of a field can be (no.) characters.

10. A field is categorized as C for _____ or N for _____. All fields designated as N must indicate the number of _____.

11. To end a system command using dBase II, type _____.

12. To add or delete a field specification within a record, type _____.

13. To retrieve a record structure, type _____.

14. To enter data, type Y when asked "Input Data Now?" or type the system command _____.

15. To change the content of a data field use the system command _____.

SOLUTIONS

1. T

2. T

3. F - This was true many years ago but is no longer true.

4. T

5. command

6. T

7. CREATE

8. F - In general, use either lower or upper case letters consistently.

9. 10; 254 (typically)

10. character (alphanumeric); numeric; decimal positions

11. CTRL W (sometimes hitting return will also work)

12. MODIFY STRUCTURE

13. USE (filename)

14. APPEND

15. REPLACE (other commands are available too)

PRACTICE ASSIGNMENTS

1. Create an Employee Data File called EMPFILE.DBF with the following format:

FLD	NAME	TYPE	WIDTH	DEC
001	SSNO	N	9	0
002	EMPNAME	C	20	

FLD	NAME	TYPE	WIDTH	DEC
003	SEX	C	1	
004	ANNSAL	N	8	2
005	DEPT	N	2	0
006	BIRTHDAT	C	8	

2. Enter the following data:

091327846	SMITH	JAMES	M	096325.21	02	01/20/44
073462721	LOPEZ	JUAN	M	073215.22	02	02/14/41
026374118	RICHARDS	MARY	F	084216.87	03	05/12/28
126327887	HAMMEL	JOHN	M	026487.32	01	06/04/51
187273221	FIELDS	MOLLY	F	038721.16	03	07/15/42

3. Display the entire file and make corrections as needed.

4. Print the file in sequence alphabetically by name, within department number. Hint: You will need to use the SORT command.

5. Print the names and salaries of all employees who earn more than $40,000.

6. Print the names of all females who earn less than $40,000.

7. Reformat the BIRTHDAT field and print the names of all employees who are older than 40.

8. Increase each employee's salary by 10%.

Data Base Management Systems Using dBase II

Figure 3.1 Important dBase II Keys

CONTROL KEYS (DOT (.) PROMPT – COMMAND MODE)

---

^P toggles printer ON and OFF   ^Num Lock   starts/stops operations
^R repeats last executed command Esc Key   aborts most operations
^X erases the current line   (Bkspc key) deletes character to left
                                                    of cursor

FULL-SCREEN KEYSTROKES (EDIT/BROWSE/MODIFY MODES)

---

^X (or cursor-down key) moves cursor to the next field or line (also ^F)
^E (or cursor-up key)   moves cursor to the previous field or line
^D (or cursor-right key) moves cursor ahead one character
^S (or cursor-left key) moves cursor back one character

^G deletes the character under cursor
   (Backspace key) deletes character to left of the cursor
^Y blanks out current field or line to right of the cursor
^V toggles between overwrite and INSERT modes
^W saves changes and returns to "." prompt

EDIT MODE
^U toggles the record DELETE mark on and off
^C writes current record to disk and ADVANCES to next record (also PgDn)
^R writes current record to disk and BACKS to previous record (also PgUp)

BROWSE MODE   MODIFY MODE
^B pans the window RIGHT one field   ^T DELETES current line
^Z pans the window LEFT one field   ^N INSERTS new line at cursor position

APPEND MODE
(cr) terminates APPEND when cursor is in first position of first field

Figure 3.2   DBase II Quick Reference Guide

The following provides an alphabetical listing of the names, functions and syntax of dBase II version 2.4 commands.

ACCEPT ("Prompt message")
TO variable
Prompts with the prompt message to enter a character string into a memory variable.

APPEND
Opens up the screen for a full-screen record add. Prompts for all fields.

APPEND BLANK
Adds a blank record to the end of the database.

APPEND FROM file
(FOR/WHILE condition)
Adds records from the named file to a database according to the specified condition if present.

APPEND FROM file
(FOR/WHILE condition) SDF
Adds records from a file in System Data Format according to the specified condition.

BROWSE
Edits several records in full screen.

CHANGE (scope) FIELD field*
(FOR expression)
Prompts with current field value. Alters the specified field(s) meeting the condition.

CONTINUE
Used in conjunction with LOCATE to point to next record meeting condition.

COPY TO file (scope) (FIELD
field*) (FOR expression) (SDF)
Copies the specified records to a database file or a System Data Format file.

FILE TO file STRUCTURE
Copies only the structure of the current database file to a new database file with no records in it.

Figure 3.2 (continued)

COPY TO file STRUCTURE
EXTENDED
Copies the structure of the current database to a database
file whose records are lines of a database structure. This
new file can be used to create a new database.

COUNT (scope) (FOR expression)
(TO variable)
Counts the number of records meeting the condition. Stores
the result in a variable if TO is specified.

CREATE
Builds a new database.

CREATE file FROM extended-file
Builds a new database using the description in the extended-
file. The extended-file is typically created by a COPY TO
STRUCTURE EXTENDED command.

DELETE (FOR expression)
Marks the specified records for deletion with an asterisk.

DISPLAY field* (FOR expression)
(OFF)
Prints the contents of the specified fields on the console
for records meeting the condition. The default is to display
only the current record. When displaying a group of records,
DISPLAY will stop after every 15 records and WAIT for RETURN
to continue. Always displays the record number unless OFF is
specified.

DISPLAY STRUCTURE
Shows the structure of the current database.

DISPLAY MEMORY
Shows the names and contents of all memory variables.

DISPLAY FILES (ON disk drive)
(LIKE shape)
Shows a file directory.

DO
Executes a dBase II command file (having the default file
extension of DMD for CP/M systems or PRG for MS/DOS systems).

EDIT n
Presents record n for full-screen updating.

EJECT
Does a form feed on the printer.

Figure 3.2 (continued)

ERASE
Clears the screen.

FIND character-string
Positions the database to the first record matching the string. The database must be INDEXED in order for FIND to work.

GOTO TOP
GOTO BOTTOM
GOTO variable n
Positions the database at the first, last, or any selected record number.

HELP command
Displays a brief explanation of the command.

INDEX ON expression TO index-file
Creates an index-file on the key expression which permits rapid positioning of the database.

INPUT prompt TO variable
Prompts for the entry of a numeric or logical memory variable.

INSERT
Enters a new record into the database at any desired position.

LIST
Works just like DISPLAY except does not stop every 15 records. LIST defaults to showing ALL records.

LOCATE FOR condition
Positions the database to the first record meeting the condition.

MODIFY COMMAND file
Invokes the dBase II editor and allows the alteration of a dBase command file.

MODIFY STRUCTURE
Alters the structure of the current database, destroying all data in the process.

PACK
Removes all records marked for deletion.

Figure 3.2 (continued)

QUIT (TO program*)
Exits from dBase II and optionally executes another series of programs.

RECALL (FOR expression)
Removes deletion status from all records marked for deletion.

RELEASE memory-variable*
RELEASE ALL
RELEASE ALL LIKE shape
RELEASE ALL EXCEPT shape
Removes the specified memory variables.

RENAME old-file-name new-file-name
Changes the name of a file in your directory. The default extension is .DBF if no extension is provided.

REPLACE (scope) (field WITH
expression)* (FOR condition)
Changes the value of the field to the expression for all records which meet the condition. The default is to change only the current record.

REPORT FORM file (TO PRINT)
(FOR condition)
Executes (or creates and executes) the report specified in the report file for those records meeting the condition.

RESTORE FROM file (ADDITIVE)
Reactivates a group of memory variables previously saved with SAVE command. Deletes all current memory variables unless ADDITIVE is used.

SAVE TO file (ALL LIKE shape)
Saves a copy of all specified memory variables into a file.

SELECT (PRIMARY)
(SECONDARY)
Changes the current database frame of reference to either PRIMARY or SECONDARY.

SET parameter (ON/OFF)
Used to alter any of the dBase configuration parameters.

SET parameter TO choice
Changes the parameter to the desired choice.

SKIP n
Positions the database either forward or backward n records.

Figure 3.2 (continued)

SORT ON field TO file
(ASCENDING/DESCENDING)
Sorts the entire database (only non-deleted records) into a new database on any single field into either ascending or descending order.

STORE expression to variable
Assigns the value of the expression to the memory variable. STORE does not work on database fields, only memory variables.

SUM field* (TO variable*) (scope)
(FOR expression)
Totals up to five fields into up to five variables for records meeting the specified condition. The default scope is ALL non-deleted records.

TOTAL ON key-field TO file
(FOR expression)
Places subtotals into a database according to the structure of the TO file. The current database must be either indexed or presorted on the keyfield.

USE file (INDEX index-file*)
Makes the specified file the current database. Two database files are permitted. Usually only the PRIMARY is used. If two data base files are needed, it is necessary to select either PRIMARY or SECONDARY with the SELECT command. If several index files are specified, only the first may be used with FIND, the others are only for updating.

WAIT (TO variable)
Suspends processing until a character is typed on the keyboard.

@ coordinates (SAY expression)
(GET variable)
Provides for custom data display and entry using full-screen editing.

? expression*
Works like DISPLAY OFF to show the value of an expression.

?? expression*
Works like ? except does not generate a new line after printing.

Note: dBase II is a registered trademark of Ashton-Tate, Culver City, CA.

CHAPTER 4

AN INTRODUCTION TO ELECTRONIC SPREADSHEETS

A. SPREADSHEET DEFINED

An **electronic spreadsheet** may be used for almost any
application where data entered in column form would be
useful, where calculations are to be performed on this data,
and where graphic output or reports based on the data would
serve a useful purpose.

The most frequently used application areas for
electronic spreadsheets include:

APPLICATIONS OF ELECTRONIC SPREADSHEETS

- Accounting
- Budgeting
- Planning
- Financial Analysis
- Modeling
- Forecasting
- Inventory Control
- Business Planning

- Income Tax Preparation
- Investment Analysis
- Property Management
- Project Management
- Tracking Sales
- Scheduling
- Billing

B. LOOKING BACK: AN HISTORICAL PERSPECTIVE

The first electronic worksheet was developed beginning
in 1978 by Dan Bricklin, a Harvard Business School student,
and Robert Frankston, a programmer. They decided that
different financial analyses frequently required similar
computations; only the actual financial data changed. They
developed the concept of a worksheet which they thought would
have widespread applicability. Along with another Harvard
student, Dan Fylstra, they formed a company called Personal
Software which later became VisiCorp. Their software package
that utilized this worksheet was called VisiCalc.

At about the same time that VisiCalc was being introduced, the Apple II computer became available. The Apple Computer Company and Personal Software worked out an arrangement whereby Apple would make VisiCalc available for its computers. This coordinated effort was probably the singlemost important development in launching the business-related PC industry. Whereas in the past, financial modeling tools were available for mainframes in the $250,000-$1,000,000 range, an Apple II together with a VisiCalc package could be purchased for under $5000. At last, the applicability and cost-effectiveness of a PC for business could be clearly demonstrated.

The initial VisiCalc spreadsheets could print data, perform basic calculations on rows and columns, interchange and replace data, copy data, reset fields, format fields, etc. More recent spreadsheets have the added capability of:

Performing advanced mathematical functions

Testing for specified conditions

Using calendar functions

Sorting

Graphics printing of bar charts, line graphs, pie charts

Advanced data retrieval

Data transfer between a spreadsheet and files created by other packages such as dBase II, WordStar, etc.

Thus, the spreadsheet has come to be a widely used, general problem-solving tool.

C. SPREADSHEETS TODAY

The more popular spreadsheet packages in use today include:

Manufacturer	Original Package (still in use)	More Recent Innovation
VisiCorp	VisiCalc	VisiOn, VisiCalc 4
Sorcim	SuperCalc	SuperCalc 3

An Introduction to Electronic Spreadsheets

Lotus	1-2-3	Symphony
MicroPro	Multiplan	Multiplan II

All of the above, as well as most spreadsheets, have a similar format. We will explain the basic rules and concepts for spreadsheet use, illustrate spreadsheets using VisiCalc, Lotus 1-2-3, SuperCalc, and some other packages, and provide a summary of rules for using the major spreadsheet packages.

The Lotus packages, 1-2-3 and Symphony, are among the more high-powered packages that have a great deal of capability. You can do many more operations with these packages than with some of the others but there is a price to pay: the command structure is somewhat more complex, particularly for the novice. Thus learning to use 1-2-3 or Symphony is more difficult than learning other spreadsheet packages, but once learned, they will provide the user with a great deal of flexibility. Note, too, that these packages make more use of the function keys, which can result in a more user-friendly focus.

Finally, 1-2-3 and Symphony have many capabilities beyond simple spreadsheeting. These include graphics capability, word processing, and data base management. Note that most electronic spreadsheets require from 64K-256K of memory; Symphony, however, requires 320K.

D. EXAMPLE 1

See Figure 4.1 for a handwritten Income Statement. To produce this Income Statement, the following calculations are required:

1. Profit = Sales - Cost

2. Expenses are a percentage of sales.

   a. General and administrative expenses are 15% of sales.

   b. Consultant fees are 12% of sales.

3. Total expenses are the sum of all individual expenses.

4. Net before Tax = Profit - Total Expenses.

5. Income Tax = 20% of Net before Tax.

6. Net Income = Net before Tax - Income Tax

We will use a spreadsheet package to create this Income statement electronically. Once created, we can make changes to determine the effects of revised formulas or different data on the final result. This is referred to as "what if" analysis and is an extremely useful tool for decision-makers.

E. THE WORKSHEET

1. Defining Cells

All electronic spreadsheets use a cell, grid, or matrix location for each item to be defined on the worksheet. When a spreadsheet is "booted" or called into storage, a blank worksheet appears which is similar if not identical to the one illustrated in Figure 4.2 which illustrates a SuperCalc spreadsheet.

Some other spreadsheets include windows with instructions or menus as well as the cells, but all have columns marked as A, B, ... and rows marked as 1, 2, 3, etc. Each cell is identified by a column, or letter, and a row, or number. A6, then, refers to the cell, grid or matrix location where A is the first column and 6 is the 6th row. The location of the A6 cell is highlighted in Figure 4.2.

The number of rows and columns permitted using a spreadsheet varies depending upon the particular package used, but the number is always more than sufficient for the novice. VisiCalc and SuperCalc, for example, allow for 16000 cells while 1-2-3 and Symphony allow for more than 500,000 cells! All packages use letters and numbers to locate a cell. AA99, for example, may be used to access a cell in a very large worksheet. Since the CRT cannot display all the cells which a worksheet may have, you will only see a small portion, or window, of the entire worksheet at any time.

When the spreadsheet is booted up, you may begin entering data at grid location A1 which is the first cell. To enter data or to "move" to any other location, you may:

1. Use directional arrow keys (↑ ←— —→ ↓) which moves you in the direction specified by the arrow.

   If you move to cells outside the window (e.g., beyond H1 to I1 or J1, for example), the window or view of the spreadsheet will change.

2. Indicate the specific location to access.

   How this is done varies from package to package. For

example, to access cell A6 using SuperCalc, you may key =
A6 or GO TO A6. In VisiCalc you access cell A6 by typing
>A6. The ">" is actually typed. In each case you must hit
the RETURN key to transmit the command. To go to a
specific location with 1-2-3 hit the F5 function key and
then type in the cell location. To return to cell Al using
most spreadsheets, hit the Home key.

The top part of the screen which is frequently boxed or
shaded is called the status area. It displays your current
cell location, the type of data being entered in that cell,
and the actual data being entered. If you make any changes to
the contents of a cell location it will appear in the status
area; once you hit RETURN, the change is made to the actual
cell or grid location.

When you boot a VisiCalc package, for example, Al will
appear in the status area since nothing has been entered yet
and the worksheet is blank.

2. Entering Constants and Formulas in a Worksheet

We may enter two types of constants or a formula in each
cell:

a. Labels or nonnumeric literals - These are constants or
identifiers. Consider Figure 4.3 which is the sample
worksheet equivalent to the handwritten Income Statement in
Figure 4.1. In Figure 4.3, the identifiers Q1, Q2, Q3, Q4
represent Quarters 1-4 and SALES represents the total of the
four quarters. These are entered in cells B3, C3, D3, E3, and
F3 respectively. They identify the contents of columns B-F.
That is, the entries in column B will pertain to the first
quarter, the entries for column C will pertain to the second
quarter, etc. Similar identifiers or constants were entered
in the A rows. The constant SALES, for example, appears as a
label or identifier in the cell labeled A5. This SALES entry
represents the total sales for each of the four quarters and
then again for the entire year.

The maximum size of a constant is typically 9
characters, unless you instruct the spreadsheet package to
increase the width of an item in a cell location. You may
also increase the width of an entire column or row to allow
for a longer identifier. /FCA15, for example, will change the
width of column A from 9 to 15 characters in SuperCalc. /F
stands for format, C for column, A for column A, and 15 for
the new length. Hit RETURN after each entry. In VisiCalc,
/GC15 will set the current column to 15 characters.

Special Features of Lotus 1-2-3

To arrive at a main menu type /. The following will be displayed on the screen:

```
A1:
                                                        MENU
-----------
|Worksheet: Range  Copy   File  Print  Graph  Data  Quit
 Global   Insert  Delete  Column-Width  Erase  Titles  Window  Status
 ┌──────────────────────────────────────────────────────────┐
 │      A         B         C         D       E       F         G           H │
|1  |
|2  |
|3  |
|4  |
|5  |
|6  |
|7  |
|8  |
 ---
```

Use the cursor arrows to arrive at the menu item desired. If Worksheet is desired the cursor is already at this first entry so just hit RETURN. If Range is desired, however, hit the ──▶ arrow once and then press RETURN.

A submenu will then appear. For example, if you choose the "Worksheet" command, the status area changes to the following:

```
A1:
                                                        MENU
--------
|Global:  Insert  Delete  Column-Width  Erase  Title  Window  Status
 Set worksheet settings
 ┌──────────────────────────────────────────────────────────┐
 │      A         B         C         D       E       F         G           H │
|1  |
|2  |
|3  |
|4  |
|5  |
|6  |
|7  |
|8  |
 ---
```

To use the menu hierarchy to change the width of column A to 15, be sure you are at column A in the grid. Then use the cursor arrows to locate the following commands and hit RETURN after each:

    /Worksheet
     Column Width

Then type 15 and hit RETURN. This will change the width of column A to 15.

Typically the top row of a column and the first column of each row of a spreadsheet contain identifiers or labels. Hence, they usually require more than 9 characters.

To enter constants you typically key in the characters you want. Once you enter a letter rather than a number, the computer considers it an identifier rather than a number. That is, with most spreadsheet packages, keying a letter as an initial character is enough to identify it as a constant. With some spreadsheet packages, however, such as SuperCalc, you must _precede_ the constant with a quotation mark to precisely identify it as a constant.

Note that with some spreadsheets hitting the ENTER key will transmit data and move the cursor to the next cell. Other spreadsheets such as VisiCalc require you to use a directional arrow to physically move to the next location.

b. Numbers - These consist of actual fixed numeric values. If the unit price of an item is 1.25, for example, you may enter this constant in its appropriate cell.

c. Formulas - In addition to entering labels or numbers, you may enter a formula in a cell. When you enter a formula, numeric values are calculated by the computer. The formula C2 * C3 may, for example, be entered where C2 is one cell and C3 is another. In this case, the computer will multiply whatever is in location C2 (e.g., UNIT PRICE) by whatever is in C3 (e.g., QTY) to obtain an amount.

3. Editing Data that has been Entered

In Figure 4.3 you could enter all numeric values as constants. Where a number, however, such as a profit of 10000 is actually determined by some formula (Sales - Cost), then it is best to use the formula. Thus, cell location B8 would contain the formula +B5 - B6.

After you have made an entry (either a label, number, or formula), hit RETURN and the computer will assume you have

Using Personal Computer Software Workbook

completed the entry. If you made a mistake go back to the cell location using the arrows and re-enter the data. You could either edit the data in a cell by calling for the edit function or fully re-enter the entire entry. /E allows you to edit an existing entry with many spreadsheets. This will bring the entry to the status area so you can work on it. You may then use cursors to move to the variable to be changed. Once you make your changes, hit RETURN to transmit them. If you change a value that is used in a formula the computer will automatically recalculate. For example, if sales for Quarter 1 should have been 30000 not 25000, you could change cell B5 by simply reentering it. B8 which is computed as B5 - B6 would automatically be adjusted, that is, B8 would contain 15000, not 10000, to reflect this change.

F. GETTING STARTED WITH YOUR SPREADSHEET

To use whatever spreadsheet package is available to you (VisiCalc, Lotus 1-2-3, Symphony, SuperCalc, etc.) you will need to follow the rules below:

1. Make sure you are using a copy of the software package (see Chapter 1 for details on making copies).

2. Use the A drive for the spreadsheet package if it contains the operating system. If not, put the operating system diskette in the A drive and the spreadsheet diskette in the B drive.

3. Determine the command for accessing the spreadsheet. Typically we use:

   VC80   for VisiCalc

   SC3   for SuperCalc3

   123   for Lotus 1-2-3 (or Lotus depending upon the specific system configurations)

   Symphony for Symphony

Suppose the VisiCalc spreadsheet package along with the operating system is on a disk in the A drive. Turn the machine on and type the following:

        A > VC80

If the 1-2-3 spreadsheet package is in the B drive and the operating system is in the A drive, turn the machine on and type:

4-8

        A > B: (to turn control over to the B drive)

        B > 123

PRACTICE ASSIGNMENTS

    Using the basic rules for entering constants and numbers
and using whatever spreadsheet package is available to you,
enter the worksheet in Figure 4.3.

1. Type VC80, SC3, 123, etc. to access your spreadsheet.

2. A blank worksheet will appear on the screen. Your status
   line will indicate that you are at cell or grid location
   A1.

3. Hit the ⟶ arrow to reach location B1. According to
   Figure 4.3 you are to enter the word INCOME as an
   identifier in B1. Type either "INCOME" or simply INCOME
   depending on what your spreadsheet manual states is
   required for entering literals. Then hit the RETURN key to
   transmit the line.

4. Hit the ⟶ arrow to reach location C1, type the word
   STATEMENT as an identifier.

5. Continue to B3 entering the identifier Q1, etc.

6. To type the actual numeric values such as 25000.00 in cell
   B5, move the cursor to B5, type the numeric value and hit
   RETURN.

NOTE: This practice assignment is designed to familiarize you
with entering constants using a spreadsheet. Later on, we
will enter formulas in place of numbers where appropriate.

G. SAVING A SPREADSHEET: A PREVIEW

    When you have completed entering the Income Statement
above as a series of constants, you will need to save it for
future processing. Each spreadsheet has a save command:

/SS	in VisiCalc
/File Save	in Lotus 1-2-3
/S	in SuperCalc

For each save regardless of the spreadsheet you will need to supply the filename. Typically you are prompted for a file name after typing the save command. The same rules typically apply for most spreadsheet filenames: 1 to 8 characters which may have an optional .extension of 3 characters. For a VisiCalc run, for example, you may type /SS INCOME.VC (.VC for VisiCalc).

REMEMBER

1. Use directional arrows to go to specific cells.

2. You can always backspace to delete characters before transmitting an entry.

3. Hit RETURN when you have completed an entry and wish to transmit it.

4. Check to see if you must precede a literal or identifier with a quote mark (") with your specific spreadsheet package.

H. PERFORMING CALCULATIONS

With some spreadsheets such as VisiCalc and Lotus 1-2-3 you can indicate a calculation by simply coding the arithmetic expression; in such cases, you must begin with an arithmetic operator (+ or -), for example. To obtain a PROFIT figure in cell location B8 for the first quarter (Q1), for example, you may code +B5 - B6 in place of 10000.00. This will result in 10,000.00 in the PROFIT grid, B8, because profit is to be calculated as SALES (25000.00) - COST (15000.00).

Using other spreadsheets such as SuperCalc you must first precede your arithmetic expression with a command such as SUM before entering the formula. This indicates that arithmetic is to be performed. The command @SUM (for sum) may not be <u>required</u> for your spreadsheet but is available as an arithmetic operator with SuperCalc, VisiCalc, Lotus 1-2-3,

Symphony, and most other spreadsheets.

Previously we indicated the formulas to actually be used in creating your income statement. We repeat them here:

FORMULAS FOR PREPARING THE INCOME STATEMENT

1. Profit = Sales - Cost

2. Expenses are a percentage of sales.

   a. General and administrative expenses are 15% of sales.

   b. Consultant fees are 12% of sales.

3. Total expenses are the sum of all individual expenses.

4. Net before Tax = Profit - Total Expenses.

5. Income Tax = 20% of Net before Tax.

6. Net Income = Net before Tax - Income Tax

PRACTICE ASSIGNMENTS

1. Load the income statement you created previously into storage. Loading a file typically requires:

   /SL filename in VisiCalc (SL = storage load)

   /File Retrieve filename in Lotus 1-2-3

   /L filename in SuperCalc (L = load)

2. Where appropriate, change constants to formulas. For example, change B8 from 10000.00, a constant, to +B5 - B6. B5 is the cell representing SALES and B6 is the cell representing COST. Change B12 (General and Administrative Expenses) to + .15 * B5 (Sales) according to the above rules.

3. Save your new INCOME STATEMENT.

I. INTERPRETING COMMON SPREADSHEET COMMANDS

Note that formulas should always be used in place of constants where appropriate. In this way, you can use the same worksheet even if SALES and COST change. Indeed, you can make projections for future sales and costs whenever you want just to see how this will affect your Profit, Expenses, and Income. This is called "what if" analysis.

We have completed the instructions necessary to produce the simple worksheet in Figure 4.3.

There are, however, many additional commands that can be used to make your worksheet more useful. To invoke any command, type / (slash) first (or use arrows to go to the specific command desired if using 1-2-3). The computer will display all the available commands in your specific spreadsheet package. Most packages use very similar commands. For example, VisiCalc will display /BCDEFGIMPRSTVW. This means /B is a command, /C is a command, etc. Figures 4.4-4.7 provide detailed information on VisiCalc, Lotus 1-2-3, SuperCalc, and Symphony respectively.

The following are among the more common commands with most spreadsheets; they are all specified below in outline form:

	SuperCalc and VisiCalc	1-2-3
Blank a Column or Row	/B	/Worksheet, then Delete
Copy Data	/C (SC only)	/Copy
Replicate Formulas	/R	/Worksheet, Global, Recalculate
Insert a Column or Row	/I	/Worksheet, then Insert

After you type the specific command, all spreadsheet packages prompt you for the rows, columns, options, etc. to use. Spreadsheets operate on the principle of main menus calling in submenus just like WordStar does. To make an insertion, for example, using VisiCalc, you type /I. The computer will then prompt you for the number of the row (R) or specific column (C) to insert.

To make an insertion using 1-2-3 you may transmit /Worksheet then Insert. That is, set the cursor at Worksheet and hit RETURN (this is the same as hitting /W). A new set of commands will appear on the screen - set the cursor on Insert and hit RETURN again. Lotus 1-2-3 attempts to be more user-friendly than older spreadsheets by including a series of prompts right on the screen.

The above commands such as blank (/B), Insert (/I), etc. used with most spreadsheets all result in computer prompts asking you for the location of the entry to be replaced with blanks, inserted, etc.

Once you become familiar with spreadsheet processing you will find that the prompts are sufficient for understanding how to proceed. Initially, however, you may need to consult a manual. Note, too, that although there are differences in the command structure of spreadsheets, there are many similarities as well.

J. REPEATING FORMULAS USING THE REPLICATE COMMAND

Frequently we wish to repeat the same formula at different cells or grid locations. For example, in the Income Statement in Figure 4.3, B15, C15, D15, E15, and F15 represent the total expenses for the first quarter, the second quarter, the third quarter, the fourth quarter, and the year, respectively. The formula placed in B15 is +B12+B13 as noted in Figure 4.3. To obtain the same summation in C15 for its corresponding expenses, C12 and C13, type /R in VisiCalc and SuperCalc, for replicate, in the B15 cell. Use /G for Global in 1-2-3, then respond to prompts. The computer will always ask you for the source range and the target range. Typically, you respond as follows:

Replicate: Source range or ENTER

<Enter>

Target Range: <C15>

Replicate N = No change, R = Relative <R>

The entries between the < > are user-supplied.

We have asked the computer to replicate or reproduce a formula at C15, the target field. The relative formula is to be +C12+C13 in place of +B12+B13. By indicating that we wish to replicate relatively, the B's are changed to C's. We can do the same thing for the D, E, and F columns as well.

K. SAVING AND PRINTING WORKSHEETS

Frequently you will want to save a worksheet so that you can make changes to it. You may want to print it as well. To print without saving, just type /P in VisiCalc and 1-2-3 for example, /O in SuperCalc. To save the file you must assign it a filename as noted previously. The rules for forming filenames are the same using most software packages including VisiCalc and SuperCalc: 1-8 characters; a 3 character extension is permitted. Typically files created using a spreadsheet would have spreadsheet identifiers automatically supplied as an extension. For example ASSETS.VC where VC stands for VisiCalc might be an appropriate filename for a worksheet. The extension .VC is automatically provided by the system when you give the file the name ASSETS.

To process a file that is stored, type /S for storage in VisiCalc, for example. The basic options to follow /S in VisiCalc are as follows:

L   Load a file or program (from a diskette to storage)

S   Save the current file on diskette

D   Delete a file from a diskette

Q   Exit from VisiCalc to the operating system (The A > prompt will appear next)

To print a VisiCalc or Lotus 1-2-3 file that contains a spreadsheet, type /P for print and then respond to the prompts. SuperCalc uses /O for output. Once again, check Figures 4.4, 4.5, 4.6, and 4.7 for details on using the most common spreadsheets: VisiCalc, 1-2-3, SuperCalc, and Symphony.

WHAT TO DO IF YOU MAKE A MISTAKE

1. If you have entered the cell already by depressing the RETURN key (⬅), then type /B to erase the cell.

2. If you have not entered the cell yet, hit the backspace key which will erase characters.

3. The scroll lock (Break) or Esc (Escape) key will typically stop any operation.

You may print a worksheet in "display mode" as in Figure 4.3 or you may print the formulas and data actually entered in each cell as in Figure 4.8.

L. "WHAT IF" ANALYSIS

Note that "what if" analysis can easily be performed using spreadsheets. That is, it is relatively easy to look at the effects of alternate assumptions. Return once again to Figure 4.3. Suppose you are the Chief Executive Officer for the company whose income statement appears in Figure 4.3. You are unhappy with the net income figures projected for each of the quarters. You may decide to do an analysis to determine what would happen, for example, if you:

1. Reduce general and administrative expenses to 11% of sales, rather than 15%.

2. Reduce consultant fees 10% of sales using Figure 1.3.

3. Reduce income taxes to 18% of net before taxes.

After loading the Income Statement, you simply go to the appropriate cells and enter the new formulas. The computer will automatically recalculate.

PRACTICE ASSIGNMENTS

1. Make the above changes using your spreadsheet package.

2. Reload your worksheet. Increase Sales by 10% and decrease Costs by 20%. Indicate how these changes affect Net Income.

M. EXAMPLE 2

1. Accessing the Spreadsheet

The following exercise highlights some of the commands and features of VisiCalc. There are, of course, comparable commands with other spreadsheets.

Type the following to access the VisiCalc package:

A > VC80

The computer will respond with a blank spreadsheet as illustrated in Figure 4.2.

2. Moving Around the Screen

1. You can move around the screen with directional arrows.

2. You can move to a specific location by keying that location. For example:

> A3

3. You can move to A1, the first cell, by depressing the home key.

3. Making Entries

At each grid location you can store:

Labels

Numbers

Algebraic expressions or formulas

Suppose you are creating a spreadsheet for a company that sells fruit. You wish to enter a spreadsheet such as the one that appears in Figure 4.9. At A3 you may type

Apples

This would be a label indicating the specifications for the number of apples sold. The Status area at the top of the screen will display:

(Entry Line)   A3

(Prompt Line)   Label

(Edit Line)   Apples

The use of letters at A3 signals the computer that the entry is a label. To transmit the entry to the computer, hit RETURN. To obtain labels for other produce, use the cursor to reach A4. For now, type "Peaches" in A4 and in A5 type "Pears".

    A4   Peaches

    A5   Pears

Suppose that for this specific month peaches are out of season. Hence the label Peaches is to be eliminated. Hit:

    /B

to blank Peaches.

To type "Oranges" in place of Peaches as in Figure 4.9, just enter the label Oranges and hit RETURN. Make the following entries as well:

    B1   Jan

    B3   56

    B4   34

    B5   29

4. Reformatting Entries

Note that when you entered Jan it appeared too far to the left on the grid. We can reformat the label so that it appears directly above the corresponding data entry as in Figure 4.9.

    B1 - To reach grid location B1 (Jan)

    /F - To reformat

The computer responds with a prompt as to what type of reformatting is necessary. The entire format D G I L R $ * stands for the following (the actual messages printed on the screen are more detailed).

    D   Default

    G   General - when numbers have different decimal
          digits

I   Round to integers

L   Left justify

R   Right justify

$ Dollars and cents

*   Values printed in graphic form

Keying R, then, will enable us to reformat with right justification. In summary, to reformat with right justification so that the label appears directly above numbers, use the entry:

/FR < >

5. Entering Algebraic Expressions

To obtain arithmetic operations, enter the formula desired. Consider the following:

+ B3 + B4 + B5 at B6

This will add the data at cells B3, B4, B5 and place the sum in cell B6 under TOTAL(A7). The word SUM can also precede an arithmetic operation if desired.

6. Copying Formulas

For Feb (Column C), Mar (Column D), etc. - we want the same summation as in Column B under B6.

/F$
/R (Replicates the formula that is the sum of 3 fields)

The computer will prompt by asking for the source range and target range.

To obtain the exact results at C6 and D6 as at B6, indicate No Change. To obtain a relative summation at C6, for example, (that is + C3 + C4 + C5 rather than +B3 + B4 + B5) hit R = relative. The following represents the prompts:

Replicate: Source range or ENTER

<Enter>

Target range <C6>

Replicate N = No change, R = relative

<R>

The entries designated within < > are user-supplied.

Once again, Figure 4.4 provides a summary of all VisiCalc options. Figure 4.5 provides a brief reference guide for similar commands using Lotus 1-2-3. Most of these are appropriate for Symphony as well. Figure 4.6 provides a reference guide for SuperCalc commands. Figure 4.7 gives an overview of Symphony.

We have provided a basic introduction to spreadsheets in general. We have also provided an overview of commands using the major spreadsheet packages.

There are numerous features not discussed here that are available to you. With this introduction, however, you should be able to read through the manual and experiment with any spreadsheet package so that you continue to increase your knowledge of it. The following is a quick review of helpful hints.

N. A QUICK REVIEW

Creating a worksheet:

1. Use the cursor control keys on the right of the keyboard to move the cursor to the desired position.

2. The spreadsheet program uses a coordinate system to keep track of entries. The columns are referenced by the letters of the alphabet and the rows are referenced by whole numbers starting at 1. For example, position B5 is directly above and to the left of position C6.

3. When you have positioned the cursor in the desired location you may begin to type in the entry. Hit RETURN when you wish to transmit the entry.

SELF-EVALUATING QUIZ

1. (T or F) Spreadsheets are frequently used for "what if" analysis.

2. (T or F) VisiPlan is a common spreadsheet package.

3. Common spreadsheet packages include _____, _____, _____.

4. All entries are placed in a _____ using a spreadsheet.

5. Locations are identified with a _____ followed by a _____.

6. To enter data in a location you may use the _____ keys or type _____.

7. The two types of values that may be entered are _____ and _____.

8. Literals are typically preceded by a _____ to identify them as literals, but this is not always necessary.

9. (T or F) +C5 * C6 + C7 might be used in a cell to perform a calculation.

1Ø. The operation to repeat a formula used in one cell so that corresponding values in another cell are similarly computed is called _____.

SOLUTIONS

1. T

2. F

3. Visicalc, SuperCalc, Lotus 1-2-3, Symphony

4. cell, grid or matrix location

5. letter; digit

   (Note: Many spreadsheets go beyond A1 ... Z1, etc. by using AA, AB, ... Hence 2 letters may precede a digit.)

6. cursor; =A6, for example, with some packages

7. literals; numbers

8. quote

9. T

10. replication

PRACTICE ASSIGNMENTS

1. Prepare an Interest table that calculates compound interest of 9.5% accrued for 10 years on a principal of 2000. Your table should appear as follows:

	A		B		C		D	
1			EARNED		INTEREST		TABLE	
2	-----------------------------------							
.								
.								
.								
15			EARNED		INTEREST		TABLE	
16								
17								
18	YEAR		BALANCE		INTEREST		ACC.INT.	
19	-------		-------		-------		-------	
20	1.00		2198.50		198.50		198.50	
21	2.00		2416.70		218.20		416.70	
22	3.00		2656.55		239.85		656.55	
23	4.00		2920.21		263.66		920.21	
24	5.00		3210.03		289.82		1210.03	
25	6.00		3528.62		318.59		1528.62	
26	7.00		3878.83		350.21		1878.83	
27	8.00		4263.79		384.96		2263.79	
28	9.00		4686.96		423.17		2686.96	
29	10.00		5152.13		465.17		3152.13	

Remember that $PN = PO(1+r)^N$ where $N = 10$, $PO = 2000$ and $r = 9.5\%$. PN = principal after N years; PO is the original principal.

2. Modify your solution to Question 1 so that the user can enter any principal, any interest rate, and any number of years.

3. Calculate the annual depreciation rate of an investment. You must provide the original price of the item, its resale price, and its age in years.

   The depreciation rate is calculated by the following

formula:

$$\text{depreciation rate} = \left(1 - \frac{\text{resale price}}{\text{original price}}\right)^{1/\text{age}}$$

(1/age is the power)

Example

Joan bought her car for $4933.76 and sold it three years later for $2400. What was its actual depreciation rate?

Empty Template:

When you are ready to enter data, the empty template will look like this:

```
   |   A    ||   B    ||   C    ||   D    |
 1 |            DEP  RATE
 2 |------------------------------------
 3 |
 4 |
 5 |
 6 |
 7 |
 8 |ORIGINAL    PRICE       =>     ENTER #
 9 |
10 |RESALE      PRICE       =>     ENTER #
11 |
12 |AGE IN      YEARS       =>     ENTER #
13 |
14 |
15 |
16 |------------------------------------
17 |
18 |            DEP RATE =>      N/A
```

SAMPLE RUN

```
     |   A    ||    B    ||    C    ||    D    |
  1|              DEP    RATE
  2|
  •
  •
  •
  7|
  8|ORIGINAL     PRICE      =>      4933.76
  9|
 10|RESALE       PRICE      =>         2400
 11|
 12|AGE IN       YEARS      =>            3
 13|
 14|
 15|
 16|------------------------------------
 17|
 18|             DEP    RATE =>      21.35
```

Figure 4.1

Income Statement		1	2	3	4	5
		Q1	Q2	Q3	Q4	Sales
Sales		25000	20000	35000	25000	105000
Costs		15000	12000	21000	15000	63000
Profit		10000	8000	14000	10000	42000
EXPENSES						
General & Admin.		3750	3000	5250	3750	15750
Consultant Fees		3000	2400	4200	3000	12600
Total Expenses		6750	5400	9450	6750	28350
Net Before Tax		3250	2600	4550	3250	13650
Income Tax		650	520	910	650	2730
Net Income		2600	2080	3640	2600	10920

Figure 4.2   Blank SuperCalc Worksheet

Figure 4.3

A1:

	A	B	C	D	E	F
1		INCOME	STATEMENT			
2		------------	----------			
3		Q1	Q2	Q3	Q4	SALES
4		--				
5	SALES	$25,000.00	$20,000.00	$35,000.00	$25,000.00	$105,000.00
6	COST	$15,000.00	$12,000.00	$21,000.00	$15,000.00	$63,000.00
7						
8	GROS.PRO	$10,000.00	$8,000.00	$14,000.00	$10,000.00	$42,000.00
9						
10	EXPENSE:					
11						
12	GEN.&ADM.	$3,750.00	$3,000.00	$5,250.00	$3,750.00	$15,750.00
13	CON.FEE	$3,000.00	$2,400.00	$4,200.00	$3,000.00	$12,600.00
14						
15	TOT. EXP.	$6,750.00	$5,400.00	$9,450.00	$6,750.00	$28,350.00
16	PRO.B. TX	$3,250.00	$2,600.00	$4,550.00	$3,250.00	$13,650.00
17	INC. TAX	$650.00	$520.00	$910.00	$650.00	$2,730.00
18	NET PROF.	$2,600.00	$2,080.00	$3,640.00	$2,600.00	$10,920.00
19						
20						

Figure 4.4 VisiCalc Commands BCDSFGIMRSTVW

The main VisiCalc menu consists of 15 commands, many of which call one or more submenus. The main menu is called by tapping the slash key (/). The following is a brief description of each Command and many of the submenus that they call.

/B Blank		Blanks the cell the cursor is currently on. Press Enter, or, move the cursor to execute.

/C Clear		Clears (erases) the spreadsheet from RAM. "Y" must be typed to confirm erasing of the spreadsheet.

/D Delete	/DIR	Deletes the row the cursor is currently on.
	/DC	Deletes the column the cursor is currently on.

/E Edit		Allows editing at the current cursor call position. While editing, the cursor arrows left and right, move a little cursor (the edit cue) on the edit line. To insert a character, simply type it in. To delete one or more characters, move the edit cue to the right and Backspace to erase. When finished, press the Enter Key.

/F Format	/FL	Left justifies cell contents of the current cell.
	/FR	Right justifies cell contents of the current cell.
	/FG	General format (maximum precision Value) / current cell.
	/FI	Integer format for Value in the current cell.
	/F$	Dollars and cents display for Value in the current cell.

/G Global	/GC	Sets new column widths throughout the spreadsheet. Column widths may be 3 characters to 80 characters in length.

Figure 4.4 (continued)

/GO   Sets order of recalculation. GOC down columns, or, GOR across rows.

/GR   Recalculation priority. GRM Turns off automatic recalc. GRA turns it on.

```
                      F

                  /   R
                          Globally   formats   the
/GF     <   Format -- G   spreadsheet to      the format
                          specified. Cells previously
                  \   I   formatted with /F are    left
                          uneffected by a global format.

                      $
```

/I   /IR   Inserts a row above the current cursor
Insert   position.

       IC   Inserts a column to the left of the current cursor position.

/M   Moves either a row or a column to a specified
Move   position. If the specified position is in the same column as the cursor, it will move the cursor's row to that position. If the specified position is in the same row as the cursor, it will move the cursor's column to that position.

/P   /PP   Prints the VisiCalc spreadsheet on the printer.
Print   Move the cursor to the upper-left cell of the area to be printed. Type "/PP". Move the cursor to the lower-right cell of what is to be printed and press the Enter key.

                To set up the printer for 132 characters/row (condensed print) type: ["^EQ(cr)] before moving the cursor to the lower-right cell position of what is to be printed.

       /PF   Prints the VisiCalc spreadsheet to a file. VisiCalc appends a .PRF extension to the filename.

Figure 4.4 (continued)

/R Replicate		Replicates a source range of cells into a target range of cells.
		To replicate a single cell into one or more cells. Move the cursor to the source cell. Type /R (Enter). Move the cursor to the first cell to be replicated into. Press the period (.) Key. Move the cursor to the last cell in that row or column that is to be replicated into and press the Enter key.
		If the source cell content is an equation, the program will prompt N=no Change or R=Relative for each cell referenced in that equation. "No Change" means the equation will be replicated with that cell reference exactly the same in all of the cells replicated into. Relative means the equation will be replicated with that cell reference dependent on the row or column of the cell it isbeing replicated into.

/S Storage	/SL	Loads a spreadsheet from a diskette into the current memory of the computer.
	/SD	Deletes (erases) a spreadsheet from the diskette.
	/SS	Saves a spreadsheet onto a diskette. Typing [LPTl:(cr)] (the device filename for the printer) in answer to the Filename: prompt will cause VisiCalc to list the cell contents of the spreadsheet on the printer.
	/SQ	Erases the current spreadsheet and VisiCalc from the computer's memory, returns to the DOS (system) level.

/T Titles	/TH	Fixes the rows up from the current cursor row position.
	/TV	Fixes the columns to the left of the current cursor column position.
	/TN	Removes the title fix.

/V VisiCalc		VisiCalc copyright notice and version number.

Figure 4.4 (continued)

/W Window	/WH	Splits the screen horizontally at the cursor row position.
	/W1	Removes the split-screen.
	/WV	Splits the screen vertically at the cursor column position.

/- Repeating label	Automatically makes a Label out of any cell entry and repeats it through the cell. Move the cursor to the position, type ; /- (the character(s), and press the Enter key.

Note: VisiCalc is a registered trademark of VisiCorp.

An Introduction to Electronic Spreadsheets

Figure 4.5   Lotus 1-2-3 Reference Guide

<u>Commands</u>   <u>Function</u>

COPY COMMAND

/C   Copy contents to new location

DATA COMMAND

/D   Operates on the spreadsheet as a database

FILE COMMANDS

/F   Use external files

C   Combine a part of a worksheet file into the
          current worksheet

D   Disk drive change to A:, or B:, etc.

E   Erase a 1-2-3 file

I   Import a standard-text into current worksheet at
          current location

L   List a directory of files and disk space

R   Retrieve and load a worksheet from disk

S   Save a worksheet into a worksheet file

X   Extract a group of cells into a worksheet file

GRAPH COMMANDS

/G   Graph the spreadsheet data

ABCDEF   Select a range of values for graphing

O   Select options for legends, symbols, etc. to be
          used in the graphs

R   Reset and cancel all previous graphic settings

T   Select the type of graph

S   Save the graph on disk for later output to the
          printer with the PrintGraph utility

V   View the graph now

Figure 4.5 (continued)

X   Define the X-range or labels

MOVE COMMAND

/M   Move the contents to a new location

PRINT COMMANDS

/P   Control printed output of spreadsheet

G   Go do the printing

P   Direct print output to Printer

F   Direct print output to File

R   Specify Range name to be printed

L   Skip to next Line on printer

P   Skip to next Page on printer

O   Set up printer options for Headers, Footings,
                Borders, Set-up Characters, Page Length, and other
                miscellaneous options

C   Cancel print settings

A   Align (reset) the line number and page numbers to
                1 after manual print.

QUIT COMMAND

/Q   Exit from 1-2-3

RANGE COMMANDS

/R   Deal with groups of cells simultaneously

E   Erase each cell of a range

F   Format numeric values for a range

I   Limit input to the range

J   Justify text in a range

N   Create, delete, or reset names of a range

Figure 4.5 (continued)

WORKSHEET COMMANDS

/W   General purpose spreadsheet manipulations

C   Adjust the individual column width of the current column

D   Delete rows or columns from the worksheet

E   Erase the entire worksheet (all data is deleted unless saved).

I   Insert blank rows or columns in the worksheet

T   Set rows or columns of titles along the edges of the sheet

S   Show current global settings and available memory

W   Create a horizontal or vertical window

G   GLOBAL

    C   Set the default column-width for the worksheet

    D   Set default printing and storage

    F   Set the default Format for numeric values and formulas for the worksheet

    L   Set the alignment of labels to either left, right, or center

    P   Permit or prohibit changes to protected cells

    R   Set order of recalculation

NOTE: 1-2-3 is a registered trademark of Lotus Development Corp., Cambridge, MA

Figure 4.6 Supercalc Commands

/B(lank), range CR

> Removes contents of all unprotected cells in specified range, or single cell.

/C(opy), range, destination cell
$$\left\{ \begin{array}{l} \text{CR} \\ \text{,N(o Adjust)} \\ \text{,A(sk for adjust)} \\ \text{,V(alues)} \end{array} \right\}$$

> Copies contents of range of cells to another address on the worksheet.

/F(format)
$$\left\{ \begin{array}{l} \text{G(lobal)} \\ \text{C(olumn)} \\ \text{R(ow)} \\ \text{E(ntry)} \end{array} \right\} \left\{ \begin{array}{l} \text{I,G,E,\$,R,L,TR,*,D} \\ \text{column letter} \\ \text{row number} \\ \text{cell address} \end{array} \right\} \text{width, CR}$$

> Changes the display format of cells, columns, rows or entire worksheet.

Format Options:

I(nteger)

> Displays numbers rounded to a whole number.

$

> Displays numbers with two digits following a decimal point.

E(xponent)

> Displays numbers in scientific notation.

Formula Adjustment Options:

Determines how cell references in formulas are adjusted for their new positions during COPY LOAD or REPLICATE. If no option is requested, all references are adjusted.

Figure 4.6 (continued)

N(o Adjust)

    Leaves all cell references unchanged.

A(sk)

    Allows specified adjustment or no adjustment of individual cell references.

V(alues)

    Moves only the current value(s) of specified cells.

/D(elete) $\begin{Bmatrix} R(ow) \\ C(olumn) \\ F(ile) \end{Bmatrix} \begin{Bmatrix} row\ \# \\ column\ letter \\ file\ name \end{Bmatrix}$

    Deletes specified cell, row, column, or range.

/E(dit), source cell, CR

    Allows editing the contents of a cell.

G(eneral)

    Displays numbers as they "best fit" into a cell.

*

    Displays numbers graphically as a string of stars.

R(ight)

    Formats numbers to be right-justified.

L(eft)

    Formats numbers to be left-justified.

T(ext)R(ight)

    Displays text strings right-justified.

T(ext)L(eft)

    Displays text strings left-justified. (Long text will continue to display in unoccupied adjacent cells.)

Figure 4.6 (continued)

D(efault)

Resets "window" (video display) to G(eneral) format. R(ight) justified numbers, and T(ext)L(eft) justified.

In addition, while formatting Global or Column, a column width or 0-127 may be specified.

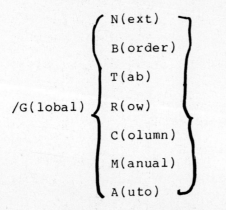

/G(lobal)
- N(ext)
- B(order)
- T(ab)
- R(ow)
- C(olumn)
- M(anual)
- A(uto)

Changes Global display or calculation options. These options affect calculation or display attributes.

CALCULATION OPTIONS:

R(ow-wise)

Specifies that calculation of worksheet be done by row; that is, all of Row 1, then all of Row 2, etc. OR

C(olumn-wise)

Specifies that calculation of worksheet be done by column; that is, all of Column A, then all of Column B

A(utomatic Calculation)

Specifies calculation of worksheet be done after each number is entered, OR

M(anual Calculation)

Specifies calculation of worksheet be done only when you enter "!".

Figure 4.6 (continued)

DISPLAY OPTIONS:

B(order)

> Controls whether or not the Row numbers and column letters are displayed (regardless of window scrolling).

F(ormula Display)

> Controls whether or not the actual formulas or the current values are displayed.

N(ext)

> Controls whether or not the cursor automatically advances (to the next cell in the "current direction") after data is entered into a cell.

T(ab)

> Controls whether or not empty or protected cells are skipped during cursor advancing.

/I(nsert) $\begin{Bmatrix} \text{R(ow)} & \text{, row \#} \\ \text{C(olumn)} & \text{, column letter} \end{Bmatrix}$ CR

> Creates a blank space for a new row or column.

/L(oad) name $\begin{Bmatrix} \text{, file ,} & \text{A(ll)} \\ & \text{P(art), source, destination} \\ & \text{range \qquad cell} \end{Bmatrix}$ $\begin{Bmatrix} \text{CR} \\ \text{N(o Adjust)} \\ \text{A(sk for adjust)} \\ \text{V(alues)} \end{Bmatrix}$

> Reads worksheet (or portion) from the disk.

> Load Options:

> A(ll)

>> Loads entire worksheet, and resets global column row formats, column widths, display mode settings, etc., from saved worksheet; OR

> P(art)

>> Loads any portion of saved worksheet into any portion or current memory worksheet. Global flags and settings are not affected.

Figure 4.6 (continued)

$$/M(ove), \left\{ \begin{array}{l} R(ow) \quad , \text{ from row \# , to row} \\ C(olumn), \text{ from column, to column} \\ \qquad\qquad\quad \text{letter} \qquad \text{letter} \end{array} \right\} \quad \text{\# CR}$$

Moves (either) rows and/or columns to a new location on the worksheet.

$$/O(utput), \left\{ \begin{array}{l} D(isplay) \\ C(ontents) \end{array} \right\}, \text{ Range,} \left\{ \begin{array}{l} P(rinter) \\ S(etup) \\ C(onsole) \\ D(isk), \text{ file name CR} \end{array} \right\}$$

Displays contents or values of cells onto the disk, console or printer.

Report Options:

D(isplay)

> Generates reports formatted in rows and columns, essentially like the interactive display.

C(ontents)

> Lists the exact contents (text or formulas), rather than current values of occupied cells, one per line.

Output Device Options:

P(rinter)

> Allows reports to be printed from the worksheet using the setup codes and page dimensions originally configured when SuperCalc was installed.

S(etup)

> Prints reports as "P", but allows special printer setup codes, or page dimensions.

C(onsole)

> Allows you to preview a report on your terminal display.

Figure 4.6 (continued)

D(isk)

     Outputs the report to a disk file for later use.

/P(rotect), range CR

     Prevents alteration of current contents in single cell, or range of cells.

/Q(uit),   Y(es)

             N(o)

     Supplies option to exit SuperCalc. This discards all worksheet data not saved on the disk.

/R(eplicate), source, destination $\begin{cases} \text{,CR} \\ \text{,N(o Adjust)} \\ \text{,A(sk for adj)} \\ \text{,V(alues)} \end{cases}$
               range   range

     Reproduces current partial rows and/or columns to another location on the worksheet.

     Options are same a C(opy)

/S(ave) $\begin{cases} \text{file name} \\ \text{CR for directory} \end{cases}$, $\begin{cases} \text{A(ll)} \\ \text{V(alues)} \end{cases}$

     Writes current worksheet data onto the disk.

Save Options:

A(ll)

     Saves text, formulas, and current values for the entire worksheet onto the disk.

V(alues)

     Saves only the text and the current values of formulas for the entire worksheet.

Figure 4.6 (continued)

/T(itle), $\begin{Bmatrix} H(orizontal) \\ V(ertical) \\ B(oth) \\ C(lear) \end{Bmatrix}$

"Locks" columns and/or rows so that they do not scroll off the window (or video screen).

Title Lock Options:

H(orizontal)

Locks current row and all rows above it.

V(ertical)

Locks current column and all those to the left of it.

B(oth)

Locks both H(orizontal) and V(ertical) simultaneously.

C(lear)

Erases all "Locks".

/U(nprotect), range CR

Allows alteration of protected data in single cell, or range of cells.

/W(indow), $\begin{Bmatrix} H(orizontal) \\ V(ertical) \\ C(lear) \\ S(ynchronized) \\ U(nsynchronized) \end{Bmatrix}$

Splits or unsplits the screen display, depending upon which command is used in conjunction.

Figure 4.6 (continued)

<u>Window Options:</u>

H(orizontal)

    Splits current screen display into two windows at current row.

V(ertical)

    Splits current screen display into two windows at current column.

C(lear)

    Erases split windows. (Return to single display window.)

S(ynchronized)

    Causes both windows to scroll simultaneously when moving parallel to split.

U(nsynchronized)

    Causes only current window to scroll, regardless of direction.

$$/Z(ap), \begin{cases} Y(es) \\ N(o) \end{cases}$$

Supplies option to erase all data from the worksheet, including Global formats and column widths.

"/Z(ap)" resets SuperCalc to original default settings.

NOTE: SuperCalc is a registered trademark of Sorcim Corp., Santa Clara, CA

Figure 4.7   Symphony Quick Reference Guide

{D}
Halts macro execution temporarily, allowing the user to type and move around; macro continues when the user presses RETURN.

{BEEP}
Sounds the computer's bell or tone.

{BLANK location}
Erases the entries from a specified cell or range.

{BRANCH location}
Continues macro execution at a different cell.

{BREAKON} and **{BREAKOFF}**
Enables and disables the use of the BREAK key to interrupt macro execution.

{CONTENTS dest-location, source-location, width-number, format-number}
Places the contents of one cell in another cell, optionally formatting the result using a particular column width and numeric display format.

{DEFINE cell1:type1,cell2:type2,...celln:typen}
Specifies cells that will store arguments specified in a subroutine call.

{FOR work-location, start-number, end-number, step-number, macro-location}
{FOR-NEXT loop}
Repeatedly executes the macro that begins at a particular location.

{GET location}
Halts macro execution temporarily and stores the character or special key the user presses as a label in a specified cell.

Figure 4.7 (continued)

{**GETLABEL** prompt-string,location}
Halts macro execution temporarily, prompts the user to type a
line of characters, and stores the characters as a label in a
specified cell.

{**GETNUMBER** prompt-string,location}
Halts macro execution temporarily, prompts the user to type a
line of characters, and stores the characters as a number in
a specified cell.

{**HANDSHAKE** send-string, receive-string,timeout-value,capture-
location}
Sends a string to a remote computer, waits a specified time
for the <u>receive-string</u>, places any response in the <u>capture-
location</u>, and branches based on success of the exchange.

{**IF** true-false-expression}
Conditionally executes the command(s) and keystroke(s) that
follow the IF command in the same cell.

{**INDICATE** string}
{**INDICATE**}
Specifies up to five characters to replace the standard
Symphony indicator in the upper right corner of the screen;
restores the standard indicator.

{**LET** location,number}
{**LET** location,string}
Stores a number or label in a specified cell. You can specify
a string-valued expression as the <u>string</u> argument.

{**LOOK** location}
If the user has typed anything, places the first character
typed at the specified <u>location</u> cell. If the user has not
typed anything, erases the <u>location</u> cell. In either case,
macro execution continues.

{**MENUBRANCH** menu-location}
Halts macro execution temporarily, prompts the user to make a
menu choice, then branches based on the choice.

Figure 4.7 (continued)

{**MENUCALL** menu-location}
Halts macro execution temporarily, prompts the user to make a menu choice, then calls a subroutine based on the choice.

{**ONERROR** branch-location, message-location}
Continues execution at a specified ranch-locationif a Symphony error occurs. Optionally stores the error message that Symphony would have displayed at message-location.

{**PANELOFF**}
Suppresses redrawing of the control panel during macro execution.

{**PANELON**}
Restores standard control panel redrawing, undoing a (PANELOFF) command.

{**PHONE** phonenumber-string}
Places a call to a specified number.

{**PUT** location,col-number,row-number,number}
{**PUT** location, col-number,row-number,string}
Stores a number or label in one of the cells of a specified range. You can specify a string-valued expression as the string expression.

{**QUIT**}
Terminates macro processing, returns control to the keyboard.

{**RECALC** location}
Recalculates the formulas in a specified range, proceeding column-by-column.

{**RETURN**}
(Subroutine return) Continues macro execution just after the location of the last {subroutine-name} or {MENUCALL} statement.

{**WAIT** time-number}
Suspends macro execution until a specified time.

Figure 4.7 (continued)

{WINDOWSOFF}
Suppresses redrawing of the windows area of the display
screen during macro execution.

{WINDOWSON}
Restores standard window redrawing, undoing a {WINDOWSOFF}
command.

Note: Symphony is a registered trademark of the Lotus
Development Corp.

Figure **4.8**

```
B1:  'INCOME
C1:  'STATEMENT
B2:  "------------
C2:  "----------
A3:  ^
B3:  ^Q1
C3:  ^Q2
D3:  ^Q3
E3:  ^Q4
F3:  ^SALES
A4:  ^
B4:  "------------
C4:  "------------
D4:  "------------
E4:  "------------
F4:  "------------
A5:  'SALES
B5:  (C2)  25000
C5:  (C2)  20000
D5:  (C2)  35000
E5:  (C2)  25000
F5:  (C2)  @SUM(B5..E5)
A6:  'COST
B6:  (C2)  15000
C6:  (C2)  12000
D6:  (C2)  21000
E6:  (C2)  15000
F6:  (C2)  @SUM(B6..E6)
F7:  (C2)  '
A8:  'GROS.PRO
B8:  (C2)  +B5-B6
C8:  (C2)  +C5-C6
D8:  (C2)  +D5-D6
E8:  (C2)  +E5-E6
F8:  (C2)  @SUM(B8..E8)
F9:  (C2)  '
A10: 'EXPENSE:
F10: (C2)  '
F11: (C2)  '
A12: 'GEN.&ADM.
B12: (C2)  +B5*0.15
C12: (C2)  +C5*0.15
D12: (C2)  +D5*0.15
E12: (C2)  +E5*0.15
F12: (C2)  @SUM(B12..E12)
A13: 'CON.FEE
B13: (C2)  +B5*0.12
C13: (C2)  +C5*0.12
D13: (C2)  +D5*0.12
```

Figure 4.8 (continued)

```
E13: (C2) +E5*0.12
F13: (C2) @SUM(B13..E13)
F14: (C2) '
A15: 'TOT. EXP.
B15: (C2) +B12+B13
C15: (C2) +C12+C13
D15: (C2) +D12+D13
E15: (C2) +E12+E13
F15: (C2) @SUM(B15..E15)
A16: 'PRO.B. TX
B16: (C2) +B8-B15
C16: (C2) +C8-C15
D16: (C2) +D8-D15
E16: (C2) +E8-E15
F16: (C2) @SUM(B16..E16)
A17: 'INC. TAX
B17: (C2) +B16*0.2
C17: (C2) +C16*0.2
D17: (C2) +D16*0.2
E17: (C2) +E16*0.2
F17: (C2) @SUM(B17..E17)
A18: 'NET PROF.
B18: (C2) +B16-B17
C18: (C2) +C16-C17
D18: (C2) +D16-D17
E18: (C2) +E16-E17
F18: (C2) @SUM(B18..E18)
```

Figure 4.9

	A	B	C	D	E	F	G	H
1		Jan	Feb	Mar	Apr	May	June	
2								
3	Apples	56	76	40	56	62	39	
4	Oranges	34	39	51	45	28	31	
5	Pears	29	42	31	38	55	48	
6								
7	Total	119	157	122	139	145	118	
8								
9								
10								
11								
12								
13								
14								
15								
16								
17								
18								
19								
20								
21								

CHAPTER 5

PROGRAMMING IN BASICA

A. Advanced BASIC for Microcomputers

This chapter of your workbook should be read after you have reviewed
chapter 12 of your textbook to obtain an introduction to BASIC programming.
Several of the ground rules set forth in the text will be used here to
illustrate optional commands, statements, and functions. BASICA is an
advanced version of BASIC designed for use on personal computers. Its
popularity is derived from ease of learning a broad scope of applications. In
fact, you will discover that it consists of many self- explanatory statements
and commands, making it easy to recall once learned. Each statement of a
BASIC program begins with a keyword or reserved word, which represents a
mnemonic of an English word. It must be preceded and followed by at least
one blank, and it may not be used as a variable name.

1. Setting up and Accessing the BASIC Interpreter

It is simple to start BASICA on the PC. First, start DOS. (See Chapter
1). Then, when you receive the A> prompt, enter BASICA. The words "Version
A" and the release number will be displayed along with the number of bytes
free. That's all there is to it. The Ok prompt lets you know the computer is
ready to be programmed.

2. Modes of Operation: Command, Execute, Edit

BASICA has three modes of operation:

```
:-----------------------------------------------------------------:
:                                                                 :
:     1  Command          2  Execute           3  Edit            :
:           Mode                Mode                Mode           :
:            :                   :                   :             :
:-----------:---------: :--------:----------:  :------:------------:
:-------------:-------: :----------:---------: :-----:-------------:
:                    :  :                   :  :                   :
: to type in programs : : to execute programs : : to edit program :
: and immediate lines : : and immediate lines : : lines           :
:---------------------: :---------------------: :-------------------:
```

Whenever the PC is in the Command Mode, it displays the OK prompt on the left
side of the screen. In Command Mode, BASIC does not accept your input until
you complete the line by pressing the return key. BASIC always ignores
leading spaces in a line -- it jumps ahead to the first non-space character.
If it is a digit, BASIC treats the line as a program line. You may enter:

   a. a program line, i.e., a line number (0 to 65529) followed by one or
      more BASIC statements or commands (separated by colons)

   b. an immediate (direct) line, i.e. one or more BASIC statements or
      commands (separated by colons)

   c. a sequence of program lines. The lines are stored in memory to form a
      BASIC program. Lines are always stored in sequence, irrespective of
      the order they were entered.

The PC executes both BASIC immediate and program lines in Execute Mode. A BASIC program is executed in ascending line number sequence, unless a control statement (GOTO, ON...GOTO, FOR/NEXT, etc.) dictates otherwise.

BASIC includes a line editor for correcting program lines. If the line is long and complicated, the Edit Mode is better than re-entering the entire line. You may enter:

a. EDIT . if you wish to edit the current line. The current line is the last line entered or edited. If while running a program an error is encountered, the line containing the error becomes the current line.

b. EDIT n where n is a specified line number. Thus, any program statement can be edited in Edit Mode.

In Edit Mode BASIC accepts your input as soon as you enter a character, without waiting for you to press the return key. Once the return key is pressed, BASIC exits Edit Mode.

The mode of operation can be changed by entering certain commands or control characters. If the PC is in:

a. Execution Mode and you press Ctrl Break while the PC is executing a BASIC program or an immediate line, execution is interrupted and the PC enters Command Mode.

b. Command Mode and you enter an immediate line, the PC enters Execution Mode.

c. Command Mode and you enter SYSTEM, the PC enters DOS and all memory is cleared.

d. Edit Mode and you press the return key, the PC enters Command Mode.

3. Entering, Listing, Saving, and Executing a Program

It is conventional to use an interval of 10 between each line number. This allows you to modify a program simply by inserting statements between lines. If your program has been prewritten on paper, the AUTO command is particularly useful, because it allows the PC to number the lines for you:

AUTO n,i   where n is the first line number generated. A period can be used to indicate the current line. The i is the interval between line numbers you want. If neither n nor i are specified, the PC starts numbering at line 10 with increments of 10. Note: if AUTO has been invoked and an * appears next to the line number, the PC is letting you know that you are writing over an existing program statement.

NEW   deletes the current program and variables from memory to allow you to enter a new program. NEW also closes all data files.

Once a program is in main memory it can be listed by using the LIST command (the listing will appear on the screen) or the LLIST command (the listing will be routed to the printer). The LIST and LLIST commands edit your programs by converting to upper case letters any reserved word (keyword, variable names, and function names) and by ordering your statements in ascending line number sequence, even though you may have entered them in a different order:

LIST n1-n2   where n1 is the first line to be listed and n2 is the last line. If a period is used in place of n1, the current line number is assumed. If only n1 is specified (and no hyphen), n1 only is listed. If n2 is not specified (and the hyphen is), the entire program is listed after n1. If both n1 and n2 are not specified, and return is pressed after the LIST command, the entire program is listed. Note: listing can be interrupted temporarily by pressing Ctrl Num Lock. Pressing any key then resumes the listing. If Ctrl Break is pressed, listing is suspended and Command Mode is entered.

A program is kept in memory only as long as the PC is switched on. If you want to retain your newly written program for future use, then you must issue a SAVE command to store it on disk. During a saving operation the disk-drive red light comes on. When it goes off, your program has been saved, and Ok appears on the screen:

SAVE f   where f is the file name or identifier that specifies the name of the program to be saved. It must be enclosed in quotation marks and may contain a disk drive identifier. For example, the command SAVE "B:MYPROG" will save the program in memory onto the disk in drive B under the filename MYPROG. If B: had not been specified, the default drive would have been assumed (the A drive unless changed while in DOS).

If the program you want to enter into memory already resides on disk, you must issue a LOAD command. LOAD deletes all variables currently residing in memory.

LOAD f,R   where f is the file name or identifier enclosed in quotation marks. R specifies that all open data files are kept open and the program is RUN immediately after it is loaded. If R is omitted (and the comma), the program is loaded into memory from disk, and all data files are closed.

Once a program is in main memory, it can be executed or "run" by issuing a RUN command. RUN will also load a program from disk and immediately run it:

RUN n   where n is the line number of your program in memory from which you want execution to commence. If n is omitted, the program starts running at the first line.

RUN f,R   where f is the file name or identifier enclosed in quotation marks. R is the same as in LOAD defined above.

During program execution following a RUN command, operation can be interrupted temporarily or aborted using a Ctrl Num Lock or the Ctrl Break press,
respectively, just as you were able to do so when listing the program.

4. Updating and Modifying a Program

       Even the most experienced programmer often needs to make changes and
corrections to a program. Your program can be updated in several ways by
deleting lines, replacing lines, renumbering lines or editing lines. Any
modification to a program in memory will close all data files and clear all
program variables from memory. Before you start to modify a program that has
been saved on disk, it must be loaded. Filenames are sometimes hard to
remember or spell. Therefore, consider using a FILES command first:

FILES f   will let you know if the file is on the disk. If the f (in
          quotation marks) is omitted, all the files on the default drive are
          presented as a directory of names. Note that a .BAS filename
          extension has been added by the PC to any program name you saved.

       It is not uncommon to save a file several times while writing a long
program. In fact, it is good practice to do so occasionally, should there be
an unexpected power failure. Sometimes the file is accidentally saved with a
misspelled file name but saved again later spelled correctly. Since the PC
does not know the first spelling was incorrect, it preserves both programs.
Or, you may want to free up disk space. If so, the KILL command can delete a
program or a data file on disk:

KILL f   where f identifies the file. If the file is a BASIC program, you
          must add the automatic file extension .BAS to the filename in order
          to kill it. For example. KILL "MYPROG.BAS" will delete the program
          saved under the filename MYPROG. Had you just entered KILL "MYPROG",
          the PC would have returned the statement "File Not Found" unless a
          data file was found under the name MYPROG.

       Deleting program lines is simple in BASIC. The DELETE command allows
you to eliminate individual lines or blocks of them:

DELETE n1-n2   where all lines between n1 and n2 inclusive are deleted. If
               the hyphen and n2 are omitted, only n1 is deleted. If n1 is
               omitted, all lines from the beginning of a program up to and
               including 2 are deleted. For safety sake, if n1 and the
               hyphen are specified but n2 is not, nothing happens.

Note: if the delete command is omitted entirely and a line number is entered
      followed immediately by return, that line is deleted.

       A line is easily replaced by another one by simply typing the same line
number and the new statement. Inserting lines between statements implies
that a new statement number be used that lies within the interval. Sometimes
the interval keeps shrinking as you continue to insert lines between
statements and eventually the interval drops to one. In this case, you have
no choice but to either retype a bundle of lines or use RENUM:

RENUM n,o,i   where n is the first line number to be used in the new
               sequence, o is the first old line number, and i is the new
               interval you desire between line numbers. If you just enter
               RENUM, the entire program is renumbered in intervals of 10.
               If you omit i, an interval of 10 is assumed. If you omit o,
               the entire program beyond n is renumbered.

Note: You will find that RENUM is one of the handiest commands around. It
      will even find a few syntax errors for you, such as when you have
      programmed the computer to branch to lines that do not exist.

      In Edit Mode you can change portions of a line without retyping it. The
PC will automatically enter Edit Mode when a syntax error is encountered
during Execution Mode. When this occurs, the PC displays the line number to
be edited and waits for you to take over:

EDIT n   where n is the line number you wish to change. If you enter a
          nonexisting line, the PC responds with an "Undefined line number"
          error. If a period is used instead of a line number, the current
          line number is assumed. Several keys are useful while editing:

      Del   delete unwanted characters without replacing them.
      Ins   insert characters while leaving all others intact.
      End   jumps the cursor to the end of the program statement.
      Right Arrow   moves the cursor to the right, one position at a time.
      Left Arrow   moves the cursor to the left, one position at a time.
      Up Arrow   moves the cursor up a row.
      Down Arrow   moves the cursor down a row.

Note: Do not use the Up or Down Arrow keys to edit a line other than the one
      you specified in the EDIT command. The PC will ignore you. Also, two
      keys cause problems. The Num Lock key can lock the num pad into numeric
      mode and destroy the End, and all Arrow key functions. Make sure it is
      deactivated. Second, the Esc erases the entire line and must be avoided
      entirely. The Home key is a nuisance also. The cursor will have to be
      repositioned using the arrow keys if Home is accidentally pressed.

5. Data Handling

Constants and Variables - Each data item may appear in a BASIC program as
either a constant or a variable. Specific numbers such a 10, -4, and 2.18 or
specific strings such as "ABC.10 or "Horse+++" are referred to as constants.
Their values remain unchanged throughout program execution. Variables are
named data items whose values can fluctuate during execution. For example,
the formula for the area of a rectangle, L*W, uses two variables, L and W, that
are reserved in a memory location for the assignment of length and width
values. The identifier name of a variable can be anywhere from 1 to 40
characters in length for unique identification. Lower case letters in a
variable identifier are equivalent to upper case and are converted
automatically to upper case when a program is listed. The first character of
a variable must be a letter. No reserved words (a keyword, a command or a
function name) can be used as a variable identifier.

Strings and Numerics - Strings are sequences of ASCII characters and are quite useful for storing non-numeric information, such as names, addresses, codes, etc. Numbers can, of course, be included within strings as well, and numerics, we will soon learn, can be converted to strings. Numeric operations (multiplication, division, etc.) cannot be performed on string data. The constant: "Harry Truman, 3rd." is a quoted string constant of 18 characters. Each character and the blank is stored as an ASCII code, requiring one byte of storage. A string constant can be up to 255 characters long. A "null" string has a length of zero and is represented by a pair of double quotes.

Numeric data can be represented in your program as either:

- Integers (speed and efficiency in processing but limited range)

- Single precision (general purpose processing)

- Double precision (maximum precision, slowest in computation).

BASIC must convert numerics to strings before it can store the information on a data file. Numbers found in strings must be converted to numerics if you have any plans on performing numeric operations on the numbers lodged in the string. Special commands are available for doing just these things.

Arrays - All variables discussed thus far are "simple variables", but the true power of BASIC is unleashed with "subscripted variables", which are elements of an "array". An array is a collection of variables of the same type under one name. You can distinguish them by the value(s) of one or more subscripts appearing in parentheses after the array name. For example, if W is a one dimensional array, W(0) is the first element, W(1) the second element, and so on. A one dimensional array resembles a list of items. A two dimensional array is like a table of values. To define an array you must:

- give it a name (any valid variable name may be assumed).

- establish the upper and lower subscripts bounds.

Both conditions are performed using a DIM statement:

DIM v(ub),v(ub)...   where v is the array name and ub is the upper bound per dimension. Several upper bounds can appear within the parentheses separated by commas. Numerous variables can be dimensioned within one DIM statement. An example best illustrates it:

10 DIM C(11),D(20,30)   Two arrays are defined here. A one dimensional array C with subscripts from 0 to 11, and a two dimensional array D with subscripts from 0,0 to 20,30.

Note: BASIC sets aside memory locations once it sees a DIM statement. An upper bound cannot exceed 255, and the product of all upper bounds within an array cannot exceed 32767. If an array variable is used without a DIM statement, the upper bound of its subscript is assumed by the PC to be 10. If the program exceeds 10 during execution, a "Subscript out of range" error occurs.

<u>Data Input</u> - There are two principal assignment statements in BASIC. A third, the LET statement is optional to use. The first is the CLEAR statement:

CLEAR ,n,m   where n sets the amount of memory available for BASIC pro-
                  grams and m sets aside stack space for BASIC. Unless your
                  programs are very complicated, both n and m can be ignored.
                  CLEAR without n and m sets all numeric variables to zero,
                  all string variables to null, and closes all data files. If
                  CLEAR appears in a program, it's like starting over.

The SWAP statement allows you to exchange the values of two simple variables. Any type of variable may be swapped but they must be of the same type (eg. string for string, integer for integer, etc.) to avoid a "Type mismatch" error:

SWAP v1,v2   where v1 and v2 are the names of two variables or array
                  elements. SWAP is really useful to speed sorting routines.

The LET statement is completely optional and in BASICA is usually used only for the sake of clarity. LET assigns a value to a variable, but note that the following two statements are identical:

```
10 LET A = X + 14
20 A = X + 14
```

A long list of data can be read by the computer from BASIC statements. The two statements set aside to handle this problem are the DATA and READ statements. DATA creates an internal data file, whereas READ reads the data from one or more DATA statements into the specified variables:

DATA c1,c2...   where c1 and c2... are numeric or string constants.
                  Expressions are not allowed in the list. DATA statements
                  can occur anywhere in the program, but READ statements will
                  access the DATA statements in line number order.

READ v1,v2...   Where v1 and v2... are numeric or string variables or array
                  elements which are to receive the value read from the DATA
                  statement. READ cannot appear without DATA. Numeric
                  variables require numeric constants; string variables
                  require quoted or unquoted strings as data. A quoted string
                  is required if the string contains commas or initial or
                  final blanks. Consider:

```
10 READ X$,Y$,Z
20 DATA "Omaha, ","Nebraska",68124
30 PRINT X$;Y$;Z
```

If this program is entered and run, the output is:

Omaha, Nebraska 68124

The DATA statement requires that you must know, when you are entering your program, exactly what values you want to assign. Furthermore, the values contained in the internal data file are saved whenever your program is saved. Hence, these values are relatively permanent because they can be changed only by changing one or more DATA statements in the program. The INPUT and LINE INPUT statements offer you more flexibility. By using them, you enter values only when the program is executed. When one of these statements is encountered, the PC suspends execution and waits for you to enter data from the keyboard. Therefore, you can write a general program to solve a particular problem before you know the specific values the program will use.

The INPUT statement allows you to enter one or more numeric or string data-items (separated by a comma). They will be assigned to the variable(s) specified in the statement. You may also include an optional prompt message:

INPUT "p";v1,v2... where "p" is a string constant used as a prompt; v1, v2, etc. are the names of variables, strings, or array elements which receive the input.

Note: A question mark is automatically displayed as a standard prompt when executing an input statement, even if "p" is omitted. The ? can be suppressed by inserting a comma after your prompt. A carriage return is echoed as well when input is executed; it can be suppressed by inserting a semicolon right after INPUT and before your prompt.

Consider the following program:

```
10 L = 20
20 INPUT "Width of rectangle";W
30 A = L * W
40 PRINT "Area is";A
50 GOTO 20
```
When this program is entered and run the output is:

```
Width of rectangle? 15          (Note: 15 entered at line 20)
Area is 300
Width of rectangle?
etc.
```

And consider another example:

```
10 INPUT;"Month and Day";D$       (Note: semicolon after INPUT)
20 PRINT ", 1985"
```
When this program is entered and run the output is:

Month and Day? November 19, 1985   (Note: November 19 entered at 10)

Responding to INPUT with too many or two few items, or with the wrong type of value (string instead of numeric when numeric is specified) causes the message "?Redo from start" to be displayed. Numeric items can be input into string variables. We will show later how they can then be converted back to numerics.

The LINE INPUT statement is particularly useful for inputting long
strings that may contain commas and significant leading and/or trailing
blanks. The maximum length of the line for input is 255 characters:

LINE INPUT "p";s   where p is a string constant serving as a prompt before
                    input is accepted and s is the name of a string variable
                    or array element that will receive the line as data.

Note: the standard prompt (?) does not appear when executing a LINE INPUT
      statement. It must be added to the prompt inside the quotes if you
      want it to appear. As with INPUT, a semicolon can be inserted right
      after INPUT to suppress the echo of the return on the screen.

Consider the following example:

```
10 LINE INPUT "Month day and year? ";D$
20 PRINT "The date is ";D$
```

When this program is entered and run, the output is:

Month day and year? November 19, 1985
The date is November 19, 1985

Note: had INPUT been used instead of LINE INPUT, the comma and everything
      after it would have been ignored. The PC would have also issued the
      error statement "Extra ignored."

And, consider removing the echo of the return:

```
10 LINE INPUT; "The date is ";D$
20 PRINT " for sure."
```

When this program is entered and run, the result is:

The date is November 19, 1985 for sure.

Data Output - To illustrate how BASIC inputs statements we gave you a peek at
one way it outputs data when the PRINT statement appeared. A number of
statements are available to allow you to output data in a standard or in a
user-defined format. The WIDTH command (or statement) can set the printer or
screen width by specifying the device and the appropriate number of
characters:

WIDTH d,s   where d is a string expression for the device identifier; s is a
             numeric ranging from 0 to 255. Valid devices are SCRN: for the
             monitor and LPT1:, LPT2: for printers. Other valid devices exist
             but are rare.

Note: Only two s values are valid for the screen, 40 or 80. The 40-column
      screen is often used for graphics and educational software. The width
      for a printer defaults to 80 when BASIC is started. Spreadsheets often
      employ condensed printing which allows large tables of up to 255
      characters wide to be printed.

WIDTH statements to handle such requirements would be:

```
10 WIDTH "SCRN:",40              (40-column screen)
20 WIDTH "LPT1:",255             (255-column printing)
```

You can use WIDTH to break up long strings containing data with a consistent pattern, thus blocking the printout. Consider the following program:

```
10 L$="111122223333344445555"
20 WIDTH "LPT1:",4
30 LPRINT L$
```
When this program is entered and run, the output is:

```
1111
2222
3333
4444
5555
```

Note: LPRINT routes output to the printer rather than the screen. We will have more to say about this next.

LPRINT l
PRINT l   where l is a list of valid expressions. PRINT displays a list of data in a standard format on the screen, whereas LPRINT routes the output to a printer. The valid expressions that follow each of them are identical. The best approach to explaining PRINT is a host of examples:

If PRINT does not end with a comma or semicolon, a new line of output is displayed when the statement is executed:

```
10 PRINT "George"
20 PRINT "Washington"
```
When this program is entered and run, the output is:

```
George
Washington
```

If no expressions appear after a PRINT statement, a blank line is printed, and the effect is a double space:

```
10 PRINT "George"
20 PRINT
30 PRINT "Washington"
```
When this program is entered and run, the output is:

```
George

Washington
```

If the list of expressions are separated by commas, each value is displayed left justified in a print zone consisting of 14 positions:

```
10 PRINT "President","George","Washington"
```

When this program is entered and run, the output is:

```
President     George        Washington
```

If one or more numeric expressions appear in a PRINT statement, then
    a. each value displayed is always followed by a space.
    b. each positive value is preceded by a space.
    c. each negative value is preceded by a minus sign.

```
10 A = 20 : P = 10
20 PRINT A * P
30 PRINT -1*A/P,A/P
```
                    When this program is entered and run, the output is:
```
 200
-2               2        (Note: the 2 appears in col. 16)
```

If a __comma__ follows the last expression in the list, the next character or
digit issued as output is displayed on the same line (space permitting).

```
10 A = 20 : P = 10
20 PRINT A * P,
30 PRINT -1*A/P,A/P
```
                    When this program is entered and run, the output is:
```
 200          -2          2
```

If __commas__ are used consecutively, the effect of each comma is to jump the
display to the next zone:

```
10 A = 20 : P = 10
20 PRINT A * P,
30 PRINT -1*A/P,,A/P
```
                    When this program is entered and run, the output is:
```
 200          -2                          2        (Note: 3rd zone skipped)
```

If __semicolons__ or blanks are used instead of commas to separate expressions in
a list, then output values are spaced more closely. Adding semicolons or
blanks adds a space. As with commas, output carries over if an expression
ends in a semicolon, but not if it ends in a blank:

```
10 A = 20 : P = 10
20 PRINT A * P;
30 PRINT -1*A/P; A/P
```
                    When this program is entered and run, the output is:
```
 200 -2   2
```

Commas and semicolons can be mixed in the same PRINT expression:

```
10 L = 20 : W = 10
20 L$ = "Length is" : W$ = "Width is"
30 A$ = "Area is"
40 PRINT L$;L,W$;W,A$;L*W
```
                    When this program is entered and run, the output is:
```
Length is 20  Width is 10   Area is 200
```
                    (Note: Convenient for labeling)

Using Personal Computer Software Workbook

Two other BASIC functions are useful when using PRINT: TAB and SPC. They will be covered when we address string functions.

Sometimes all you want to do is take a quick look at your data without much regard for appearance. The WRITE statement handles it nicely:

WRITE l   where l is a list of expressions separated by a comma. They may be numeric, string, relational or logical. Strings will be delimited by quotation marks, and each item will be separated by a comma when displayed:

```
10 L = 20 : W = 10
20 A$ = "Area is"
30 WRITE L,W,A$,L*W
```
When this program is entered and run, the output is:

20,10,"Area is",200

As you can see, WRITE is a "brute force" data output statement. On the other hand, PRINT USING or LPRINT USING are designed for making things look good when they are displayed (again, the L just means that your printer is involved). The format of your output is, therefore, user-defined. Options are numerous. The expressions in a PRINT USING statement must be separated by commas or semicolons (makes no difference which), and values will be output in a format specified by the expression after USING. A host of formatting characters determine the fields and the format of the output strings or numerics.

PRINT USING "s";l   where s is a string of formatting characters or a string variable consisting of a string of formatting characters; l is a numeric, relational, logical or string expression which is to be displayed. The statement is best explained with several examples.

First, let us examine strings. If the formatting characters is a ! then only the first character in a given string will be output:

```
10 A$ = "George" : B$ = "Washington"
20 PRINT "The first President's initials are ";
30 PRINT USING "!";A$;B$
```
When this program is entered and run, the output is:

The first President's initials are GW

If the formatting character is \n spaces\ then 2+n characters from the string will be output. If the backslashes are entered with no spaces, two characters will be output; with one space, three characters will be output; and so on:

```
10 A$ = "George" : B$ = "Washington"
20 PRINT USING "\ \";A$;"\  \";B$
```

When this program is entered and run, the output is:

GeoWash

5-12

If the formatting character is an & then the entire string is printed exactly
as it was input. This works well when used after ! or \\ in the same PRINT
USING statement to effectively cancel them:

```
10 A$ = "George" : B$ = "Washington"
20 PRINT USING "!";A$;"&";B$
```

When this program is entered and run, the output is:

GWashington

Now, let us consider what we can do with numerics. If the formatting
character is a # then space is set aside to pack the digits into a field
defined by the number of #s indicated. Numbers are right justified. If the
data has more numbers than #s, the data is rounded. Blanks can be used
inside the quotes to provide spacing:

```
10 A = 1234.5 : B = 67
20 PRINT USING " ####   ";A;B
```

When this program is entered and run, the output is:

   1234   67

In addition, a decimal point can be added so that the same number of digits
to the right of it will always appear. Zeros are added to the right of the
decimal when necessary, and blanks are padded to the left. Let's use a loop
to show how well things get lined up:

```
10 DATA 12.1234,-1.50,9456.1,357
20 FOR I=1 TO 4
30  READ A(I)
40  PRINT USING "####.##";A(I)
50 NEXT I
```

When this program is entered and run, the output is:

```
   12.12
   -1.50
 9456.10
  357.00
```

(Note: this is really helpful for spreadsheets. Study
the padding, rounding and aligning.)

A plus sign appearing before the first # or after the last # will force both
plus and minus signs to appear before or after, respectively:

```
10 DATA 12.1234,-1.50,9456.1,357
20 FOR I=1 TO 4
30  READ A(I)
40  PRINT USING "+####.##";A(I)
50 NEXT I
```

When this program is entered and run, the output is:

```
  +12.12
   -1.50
+9456.10
 +357.00
```

If a minus sign is placed after the last # then negative numbers will appear
with a trailing minus sign:

```
10 DATA 12.1234,-1.50,9876.1,357
20 FOR I=1 TO 4
30   READ A(I)
40   PRINT USING "####.##-";A(I)
50 NEXT I
```
                    When this program is entered and run, the output is:
```
  12.12
   1.50-                (Note: in a long column, the negative numbers stand
9876.10                        out very well to highlight them.)
 357.00
```

A double asterisk ** before the first # causes all leading spaces to be
filled with ** instead of blanks. Each * also allows room for another digit:

```
10 DATA 12.1234,-1.50,9876.1,357
20 FOR I=1 TO 4
30   READ A(I)
40   PRINT USING "**##.##";A(I)
50 NEXT I
```
                    When this program is entered and run, the output is:
```
**12.12
**-1.50
9876.10                (Note: very useful for highlighting small numbers.)
*357.00
```

If a $$ appears prior to the first # then a dollar sign will appear to the
immediate left of the number, preceded by one blank space. Negative numbers
are lost unless the - appears to the right of the last #:

```
10 DATA 9876.1,-1.50
20 FOR I=1 TO 2
30   READ A(I)
40   PRINT USING "$$####.##-";A(I)
50 NEXT I
```
                    When this program is entered and run, the output is:
```
 $9876.10
    $1.50-
```

The ** can be combined with a single $ to fill all leading blanks with an *
and finally a $:

```
10 DATA 9876.1,31,.68
20 FOR I=1 TO 3
30 READ A(I)
40 PRINT USING "**$####.##";A(I)
50 NEXT I
```
                    When this program is entered and run, the output is:
```
$9876.10
**$31.00
****$.68
```

When you run into large numbers, a comma to the left of the decimal point
will trigger the standard convention of inserting a comma in the display
every third digit:

```
10 DATA 123456789.7,23,1234.56
20 FOR I=1 TO 3
30  READ A(I)
40  PRINT USING "$$##########,.##";A(I)
50 NEXT I
```

When this program is entered and run, the result is:

```
$123,456,789.70
       $23.00
    $1,234.56
```

(Note: $$ has been added to show that both can be
combined in the same expression).

You can even convert all your data to exponential format by using ^^^^ placed
after any of the # that are left of the decimal. Significant digits are left
justified and the exponent is adjusted accordingly. An extra # will be needed
for displaying digits to the left of the decimal.

```
10 DATA 98764,-33.55,452.7
20 FOR I=1 TO 3
30  READ A(I)
40  PRINT USING "##.###^^^^";A(I)
50 NEXT I
```

When this program is entered and run, the result is:

```
 9.876E+04
-3.355E+01
 4.527E+02
```

Virtually anything on the keyboard can be displayed along with the numeric if
an underscore precedes the first # or trails the last # (even the underscore
itself), followed by the character to be shown:

```
10 DATA 367.122,327.0,.56
20 FOR I=1 TO 3
30  READ A(I)
40  PRINT USING "_@###.##_%"
50 NEXT I
```

When this program is entered and run, the result is:

```
@367.12%
@327.00%
  @.56%
```

If the percent sign shows up in front of a number after you have used PRINT
USING, it means the number to be displayed is larger than the numeric field
you set aside to show it. Rounding up can also cause it:

```
10 A = 67.5:B = 9.99
20 PRINT USING "#.##";A;B
```

When this program is entered and run, the output is:

```
%67.50 %10.00
```

(Note: an error has been detected in both cases.)

String Functions - String statements and/or functions can do the following:

a. return a string from a numeric value.
b. convert a numeric value into a string.
c. permit one or more numeric and/or string arguments.
d. simplify string operations by extracting characters from a larger string.

Using string statements, you can exert maximum control over the PC's ability to display practically anything on the screen or to store and retrieve data. Let's first consider ASC:

x = ASC(x$)   where x becomes a numerical value that is the ASCII code of the first character of the string x$. The PC has 255 ASCII characters, each defined by a numeric. Let's look at four of them:

```
10 DATA Able,Baker,Charlie,Dog
20 FOR I=1 TO 4
30   READ A$(I)
40   PRINT ASC(A$(I));
50 NEXT I
```
                    When this program is entered and run, the output is:
 65 66 67 68

The antithesis of the ASC function is the CHR$ function, which returns a one-character string whose ASCII code is the value of the argument.

x$ = CHR$(x)   where x is evaluated and rounded to the nearest integer. It must be in the range of 0 to 255, otherwise an "Illegal function call" error occurs:

```
10 FOR I=34 TO 37
20   PRINT CHR$(I),
30 NEXT I
```
                    When this program is entered and run, the output is:

"   # $ %   &

Note: CHR$ is commonly used to send special characters to the terminal, or it can even be used to inspect strings for the presence of specific characters. How? Just keep reading.

The PC will "read" a character you enter from the keyboard as a string and use it to do whatever you want. Consider the INKEY$ function:

x$ = INKEY$ where x$ is read immediately from the keyboard without displaying anything. A null string indicates no characters are pending (nothing has been pressed). Consider this example:

```
10 A$=INKEY$: IF A$="" THEN 10          Statement 10 freezes everything
20 IF A$ <> "h" THEN 40                 until you press a key.
30 PRINT "Hello "
40 PRINT "Dolly"          Pressing the h key prints Hello Dolly.  Any
                          other key displays Dolly alone.
```

You can specify the length of the string picked up from the keyboard before anything is performed by the PC. Using the INPUT$ function, no characters are echoed as you key them in, but the machine "reads" them anyway:

x$ = INPUT$(n)   where n is the length of the string being keyed in, rounded to the nearest integer (maximum = 255). Let's input four 6-character strings as fast as possible:

```
10 FOR I=1 TO 4
20  A$(I)= INPUT$(6)
30  PRINT A$(I)
40 NEXT I
```
        Only after 6 characters are keystroked will the PC print the 6-character string. Nothing occurs until then. Without having to press the return key, the next string can be keyed in.

Note: INPUT$ is valuable when you must enter loads of data from the keyboard and the return key need not be pressed. Experts on the numeric pad do not need to see the echo on the screen, and the return key is usually a nuisance to them.

    Strings have lengths, and characters are positioned within them. Here is how we can find the characters and use the length of the string:

x = INSTR(n,x$,y$)   where n is the start position, a numeric expression rounded to the nearest integer which specifies where the search is to begin. If omitted, 1 is assumed. x$ is the "parent" string; y$ is the substring whose first occurrence is being investigated:

```
10 X$ = "George Washington"
20 Y$ = "Wash"
30 PRINT INSTR(4,X$,Y$)        (Note: the search will start at the r).
```

            When this program is entered and run, the output is:
 8

If the starting position, n, falls outside the range of 1 to 255, you will receive an "Illegal function call" error. If the substring cannot be found, or if you specified a substring longer than the parent string, the returned value is 0.

The length of a string can be measured using the LEN function:

x = LEN(x$)   where x$ is any string expression with a length of x:

```
10 X$ = "George Washington"
20 X = LEN(X$)
30 PRINT X
```
            When this program is entered and run, the output is:
 17
Note: all characters are counted, including blanks. A null string has a length of zero, and if the return key only was pressed after an INPUT statement, that string remains a null.

Three functions allow you to partition strings and create substrings: LEFT$, RIGHT$ and MID$. LEFT$ returns a substring comprised of the leftmost characters of a parent string:

s$ = LEFT$(x$,n)   where x$ is the parent string and s$ is the substring of length n. The length n is a numeric expression rounded to the nearest integer within the range from 0 to 255. If n exceeds the length of the parent string, the parent string is returned:

```
10 A$ = "George Washington"
20 B$ = LEFT$(A$,6)
30 PRINT B$
```
When this program is entered and run, the output is:

George

The RIGHT$ function is the counterpart of LEFT$. RIGHT$ returns a substring comprised of the rightmost characters of a parent string:

s$ = RIGHT$(x$,n)   where all terms are the same as defined for LEFT$ above:

```
10 A$ = "George Washington"
20 B$ = RIGHT$(A$,10)
30 PRINT B$
```
When this program is entered and run, the output is:

Washington

The MID$ returns a substring from a parent string, starting from a specified character position. The length of the substring can be specified, or all the characters to the end of the string are returned.

s$ = MID$(x$,n,m)   where x$ is the parent string from which the substring s$ is derived, starting with the n character position of x$ and ending with the m character position. If m is omitted, all characters to the end of x$ are returned.

```
10 A$ = "George Washington Carver"
20 B$ = MID$(A$,8,10)
30 PRINT B$
```
When this program is entered and run, the output is:

Washington

There are three functions that allow you to manipulate strings and numerics and convert from one to the other. First, consider STR$:

x$ = STR$(x)   where x is any numeric expression. The returned string, x$, contains a leading blank plus all the characters included in x.

```
10 X = 15*20
20 PRINT STR$(X)
```
When this program is entered and run, the output is:

 300

The counterpart to the STR$ function is VAL. The VAL function converts a
string representation of a number to its numeric value. From there on,
numeric operations can be performed on the data.

x = VAL(x$)   where x$ is a string expression being evaluated and converted
                to the numeric equivalent x:

```
10 A$ = "               68124"
20 PRINT VAL(A$)
```
                    When this program is entered and run, the output is:
```
 68124
```

Another useful string function is appropriately named STRING$. You can use
STRING$ to create a string of specified length, whose characters are all the
same specified ASCII code value or are all the first character of another
string:

s$ = STRING$(n,m)
s$ = STRING$(n,x$)   where n is a numeric expression from 0 to 255 that
                        sets the length of s$. m specifies an ASCII decimal
                        code from 0 to 255 whose equivalent character forms
                        s$. The first character of x$ is used to form s$.

```
10 A$ = "George Washington"
20 B$ = STRING$(9,42)
30 C$ = STRING$(10,A$)
40 PRINT B$;C$
```
                    When this program is entered and run, the output is:
```
*********GGGGGGGGGG
```

Positioning data to be displayed is facilitated by two commonly used
functions: TAB and SPC. Both must be used with the PRINT or LPRINT
statements to position the cursor (or print head):

PRINT TAB(n)
LPRINT TAB(n)   where n is a numeric expression from 1 to 255. Outside
                    this range produces an "Illegal function call" error. If
                    the current cursor or print head position is beyond n
                    already, then TAB jumps to that position on the next line.

```
10 DATA New Shoes,1 pair,$35.00
20 READ A$,B$,C$
30 PRINT "ITEM";TAB(15)"QUANTITY";TAB(30)"PRICE"
40 PRINT A$;TAB(15)B$;TAB(30)C$
```

                    When this program is entered and run, the output is:

```
ITEM            QUANTITY        PRICE
New Shoes       1 pair          $35.00
```

Note: had any of the strings been longer than 15 characters TAB would have
      moved everything after that string to the next line.

The SPC function inserts spaces in PRINT or LPRINT statements:

PRINT SPC(n)
LPRINT SPC(n)   where n is a numeric expression from 0 to 255 specifying
                       the number of spaces to be inserted at the beginning,
                       between two items being displayed, or at the end:

PRINT SPC(5);"JUMP";SPC(10);"10 SPACES"
     JUMP   10 SPACES

The SPACE$ function is so closely related to the SPC function that it should
be mentioned here:

x$ = SPACE$(n)   where n is a numeric expression from 0 to 255 which
                       specifies the number of blank spaces, and hence the length
                       of x$, which contains only blanks:

```
10 DATA 5,10,15,20
20 FOR I=1 TO 4
30   READ A(I)
40   PRINT SPACE$(A(I));I
50 NEXT I
```
                              When this program is entered and run, the output is:

     1
            2
               3
                   4

Debugging and Error Recovery - Now, let us leave string functions alone for
awhile and switch gears. As humans we make errors. BASIC has some very
friendly ways of helping us deal with them. Even accomplished programmers
can rarely write an error-free program at first attempt. There are, in
general, two-types of errors that can be made:

 - run-time errors, which halt execution and cause an error message. They
   may be Syntax errors (when a statement contains some incorrect sequence of
   characters) or other types of run-time errors (NEXT without FOR, RETURN
   without GOSUB, etc...). You can also simulate the occurrence of a BASIC
   error, or generate a user defined error type (to be handled by an error
   trap routine).

 - logic errors, which permit complete execution but cause incorrect or
   unexpected results. These errors are the most difficult to find. Assume,
   for example, you have written a program that is supposed to print the
   results of 15 calculations. When the program is run, only 11 results are
   obtained. If the program is long and complex, with many branches, loops
   and subroutines, finding an error is not a simple task. You could have
   gone wrong in many ways, and statements must be traced. It would be
   particularly helpful in correcting logic errors if you knew exactly which
   statements are being executed - and when.

The PC provides a number of features within BASIC that reduce the cost and frustration of debugging. A convenient method of debugging logic errors is to trace the order of statement execution in all or part of a program. Two tracing commands (also usable as program statements) are available:

TRON   (TRACE ON) causes the line number of each statement to be listed as it is executed. Each line number of the program is displayed as it is executed, enclosed in a pair of brackets.

TROFF   cancels TRON like a toggle switch.

```
10 TRON
20 DATA TRON ,is,activated.
30 FOR I=1 TO 3
40   READ A$(I)
50   PRINT I;A$(I)
60 NEXT I
70 TROFF
```
                    When this program is entered and run, the output is:

```
[20][30][40][50] 1 TRON        (Numbers which are not enclosed in square
[60][40][50] 2 is               brackets are the output of the PRINT I;A$(I)
[60][40][50] 3 activated.       statement.)
[60][70]
```

The END statement is not required in a BASIC program (note that none of our examples thus far include it) but it performs useful functions:

END   a stand-alone command that closes all open files and enhances readability. It may be placed anywhere in the program to end the program if some condition is met. The PC returns immediately to Command Mode once END is encountered.

Note: END does not erase variables from memory. You can print the values of any program variables by an immediate PRINT or PRINT USING statement.

STOP   is similar to pausing while in progress. Like END, a STOP statement can be used anywhere in the program, but when encountered, the PC displays: "Break in line nnnnn" to let you know where it is. Also, data files remain open. PRINT can be used again to show values of variables in memory. But, unlike END, execution can be resumed right where it left off by issuing a CONT command:

CONT   continues program execution after Ctrl Break was entered from the keyboard or after a STOP statement was encountered in the program. If any line is edited, however, CONT is invalid.

    Run time errors normally halt execution and cause a standard error message to be displayed. Through use of the ON ERROR GOTO statement, error handling routines can be entered so that execution continues with the specified line after an error occurs. The ON ERROR GOTO needs to be executed only once (and usually early) in the program to enable error trapping. The power of ON ERROR GOTO cannot be realized without using it in conjunction with ERROR, ERR, ERL and RESUME:

ERROR n   where n is an integer expression between 0 and 255 which
                 represents an error code. ERROR simulates the occurrence of a
                 BASIC error, or generates a user-defined error.

  - If the value of n equals an error code already in BASIC, the ERROR
    statement will simulate the occurrence of that error, and the
    corresponding error message will be displayed.

  - If the value of n is greater than any used by BASIC error codes, the ERROR
    statement will generate a user-defined error which may then be handled in
    an error trap routine setup by ON ERROR GOTO. If n > 73, conflict with
    BASIC error codes will be avoided.

  - If an ERROR statement specifies a code for which no error message has been
    defined, the PC responds with the message: "Unprintable error."

The ON ERROR GOTO statement enables error trapping and specifies the first
line of the error handling routine. A program can contain only one error
handling routine unless CLEAR is encountered and a new routine is
constructed:

ON ERROR GOTO l   where l is the first line of the error handling routine.
                   If l is 0 then error trapping is disabled. Once enabled,
                   all errors detected will cause a jump to the specified
                   error trap routine. If an error occurs within the error
                   trap routine, the BASIC error message is displayed and
                   execution terminates.

A fool-proof error trap still needs ERL and ERR:

c = ERR
l = ERL   where c is the error code returned by ERR and l is the line
                 number of the line in which the error was detected. Both ERL
                 and ERR functions are usually used with IF...THEN to direct
                 program flow in the error trap routine. They are also best used
                 in conjunction with RESUME:

RESUME l
RESUME NEXT   where program execution resumes at the specified line number l
                 or at the NEXT statement (after the one which caused the
                 error). RESUME must be within an error trap routine setup by
                 ON ERROR GOTO, otherwise a "RESUME without error" message will
                 appear. Consider this example which ties everything together:

```
100 ON ERROR GOTO 200                       (Error trap enabled.)
110 INPUT "Place your bet";B
120 IF B > 5000 THEN ERROR 210              (Error number established.)
 .
 .
200 IF ERR = 210 THEN PRINT "House Limit is $5000"
210 IF ERL = 120 THEN RESUME 110                      (Return for valid input.)
220 ON ERROR GOTO 0                          (If reached, some other error was
                                              encountered.  Program halts.)
```

B. DISK FILE HANDLING

A data file is created by an OPEN statement which allows a BASIC program to access the file. Two major types of files can be opened: sequential and random. Sequential files permit three different access modes (Input, Output and Append), whereas random files permit only one access mode (Random). The access mode may be changed for a file each time it is opened.

1. Sequential and Random File Characteristics

a. Sequential - a stream-oriented file that is a sequence of ASCII characters without any grouping criterion. The number of data items read or written by each Input/Output statement can vary.

b. Random - a sequence of data grouped on records of pre-specified length. Each Input/Output statement may read or write one record at a time.

Sequential files are the simplest way to store data. They are ideal for storing free-form data (which may not be grouped in records). The data that is written to a sequential file is stored, one item after another (in sequence), in the order it is sent and is read back in the same order. If you decide to:

- open a sequential file in Output, you start writing at the beginning of the file and the file's previous contents are erased.

- open a sequential file in Append, you start writing after the last data item on the file.

- update a sequential file, open the file in Input, read the file and write the updated file to a new file which must have been opened in Output.

- read a sequential file, you must open it in Input.

- write data to a sequential file, only strings can be used.

Random files require more program steps to access, but there are advantages when using them:

- instead of having to start reading or writing at the beginning of a file, you can read or write any record you specify.

- to update a random file, you do not have to read the entire file, update the data and write it again. You can rewrite or add to any record you choose, without accessing the preceding records.

2. Opening and Closing Files

To access a file with a BASIC program, you must open it with an OPEN statement. This specifies the file identifier, the access mode, the file number and if the file is a random file, the record length. Unless reset by DOS, only three files may be open at the same time in the program. Whenever

you open a file, a buffer number is associated with the file. This is a waiting
area of memory that data must pass through on the way to and from the disk
file. Two modes exist for the OPEN statement:

OPEN f FOR m AS fn LEN=r
                        alternatively:
OPEN m2,fn,f,r

> where f is the file specification, fn is the file (buffer)
> number, and r is the record length (required only for random
> files). The access mode, m, must be one of these keywords:
> OUTPUT - for sequential output mode.
> INPUT - for sequential input mode.
> APPEND - for sequential output after the last data item.
> If the alternate format is selected, m2 must be either:
> "A" for appending; "I" for input; "O" for output if the file
> is sequential. "R" is used in all instances for random files.

Any of the following are valid OPEN statements for sequential files:

10 OPEN "SEQFILE" FOR OUTPUT AS 1   (Sequential file opened for output mode)
20 OPEN "DATA" FOR INPUT AS 2   (Sequential file opened for input mode)
30 OPEN "FILE" FOR APPEND AS 3   (Sequential file opened for append mode)

> The same three statements using the alternate format:

10 OPEN "O",1,"SEQFILE"
20 OPEN "I",2,"DATA"
30 OPEN "A",3,"FILE"

Here are two valid statements for opening a random file:

10 OPEN "RANFILE" AS 1,80   (Note: FOR is not required; record length 80
                                  is required.)

> The same statement using the alternate format:

10 OPEN "R",1,"RANFILE",80

Note: DOS defaults to a maximum record length of 128 characters. It can be
      reset when BASICA is first accessed, to as high as 32767. Suppose you
      want to open four files and need a record length of 512. From the DOS
      A>, enter the following command: BASICA/F:4/S:512

Usually three files are all you need to have open at once. If you are going
to manipulate more than three in the same program, consider closing the ones
you do not need to have open as the program moves along:

CLOSE 1,2...   where 1, 2, etc. are file numbers matching those used to open
                the files originally. If 1, 2, etc. are omitted, all files
                are closed.

Note: If a CLOSE is executed, the buffer may now be reused to OPEN any file
      using the same buffer number.

A closed file can be reopened within the same program using any free buffer number available. If the file is reopened with a number that has been assigned to another file, BASIC will respond with a "File already open" error message. If an attempt is made to close a file already closed, BASIC ignores the fruitless attempt. It is usually good practice to close a file when you are through with it.

3. Reading a Sequential File

To read a sequential file, you must open it in Input mode ("I"). The INPUT and LINE INPUT# statements allow you to read data from a sequential file. INPUT# reads one or more data items separated by delimiters and assigns them to numeric and/or string variables. LINE INPUT# reads an entire line and assigns it to a string variable. You will also find two BASIC functions, EOF and LOC, very helpful when dealing with sequential files:

- EOF allows you to test whether an end of file condition exists to suspend all reading operations and prevent the error message "Input past end."

- LOC tells you the number of sectors (256 byte blocks) read from the file since it was opened.

Let us first consider the INPUT# statement:

INPUT# fn,v1,v2... where fn is the file number associated with the file; v1, v2, etc. are names of variables which will receive a data item from the file.

Study these characterstics:

- When INPUT# is executed, data is input sequentially from the beginning of the file. Each time a data item is input (a delimiter is reached), the pointer moves to the next data item. To restart reading the file, it first must be closed and then reopened.

- If you want to input data successfully, you must know the type (numeric or string) of each successive data item on the file. Data items must be separated by delimiters.

- Numeric items from the file may be input as strings and then converted later to numerics using VAL.

- If BASIC is inputting a numeric variable, all leading spaces, carriage returns and line feeds are ignored. The first character encountered that is not one of these is read as the start of the number. The number then terminates when a space, carriage return, line feed, or comma appears.

- If BASIC is inputting a string variable, all leading spaces, carriage returns and line feeds are also ignored. The first character encountered that is not one of these is read as the start of a string. If the first character is a quotation mark, the string consists of all characters between the first quote and the second. Thus, quoted strings may not contain quotation marks.

- If the first character is not a quotation mark, the string is an unquoted
  string and will terminate with either a comma, carriage return or line
  feed (or after 255 characters have been read).

For example, suppose your data on the file is as follows:

Strings, Strings "and more strings."

INPUT#1,A$,B$,C$ will yield: A$ = Strings
                                   B$ = Strings "and more strings."
                                   C$ = null string

But if the data on the file is:

Strings, Strings, "and more strings."   (Note: comma inserted)

The same INPUT# statement yields: A$ = Strings
                                  B$ = Strings
                                  C$ = and more strings.

Delimiters are ignored, thus permitting quotation marks, blanks, etc. to be
read everywhere when you use the LINE INPUT# statement:

LINE INPUT# fn,x$ where fn is the file number under which the file was open
                      and x$ is a string variable assigned to an entire line
                      (up to a carriage return) with a maximum of 254
                      characters. Numerics cannnot be read directly.

Consider these characteristics:

- If a LINE INPUT# statement is executed, all characters are read in the
  file until one of the following is encountered:
    a. a carriage return or carriage return/line feed sequence.
    b. the end of the file is reached.
    c. the 254th data character is found (and included).

- If leading characters or other delimiters are encountered (quotes, commas,
  blanks, etc.), they are included in the string. The MID$ function may
  have to be used to clean up the display.

EOF and LOC are usually used in conjunction with an IF statement. EOF will
suspend reading to prevent an "Input past end" error and continue program
execution. LOC can be used to stop reading when a specified quantity of the
file has been read (valuable for large files):

EOF(fn)
LOC(fn)   where fn is the file number in either function. Both can be used
          with random files as well. LOC returns the number of 128 byte
          blocks that have been read from (or written to) on a sequential
          file. LOC returns the record number of the last one read from (or
          written to) on a random file. LOC returns a 1 before any data has
          been read.

The following example illustrates how a sequential file can be read:

```
10 OPEN "I",1,"DATA1"
20 FOR I=1 TO 1000          Reads 1000 data items.
30  IF EOF(1) THEN 80        Checks for end of file.
40  IF LOC(1) > 50 THEN 80   Limits reading to 50 blocks.
50  INPUT#1,X$               Reads the data as string.
60  PRINT X$                 Displays the data on the screen.
70 NEXT I
80 PRINT LOC(1)*128;"bytes were read from the file."
90 CLOSE : END
```

4. Writing a Sequential File

To write a sequential file you must OPEN it in output ("O") or Append ("A"). Output statements are PRINT#, PRINT# USING and WRITE#. PRINT# and WRITE# output standard format data, whereas PRINT# USING outputs data in a user defined format. The difference between PRINT# and WRITE# is that:

- PRINT# writes data to disk in the same format used by the PRINT statement.

- WRITE# writes data to a disk in the same format used by the WRITE statement, i.e., inserting commas between data and quoted string values.

PRINT# fn,exp   where fn is the file number used when the file was opened and exp is a list of expressions defining the data to be written to the file. The expressions can be numeric, relational, logical or strings. Study these characteristics:

- If the file is opened for Output ("O"), the file pointer is set at the beginning of the file. For each PRINT# operation, the pointer advances to write the values in sequence.

- If the file is opened for Append ("A"), the file pointer is set at the end of the file. Each PRINT# operation advances it from there.

- You should set up your PRINT# list of expressions for access by one or more INPUT# statements, recognizing that PRINT# creates a disk image similar to the way PRINT creates a screen image. Punctuation is crucial, because unquoted commas and semicolons have the same effect as they do in PRINT statements.

- If you intend to output numeric values, you may use either commas or semicolons to separate the expressions. Semicolons save disk space.

- If you have to output string values, insert explicit delimiters in order to INPUT# them as distinct strings.

- Suppose you have to output string values which do not contain commas, semicolons, significant leading or trailing blanks, carriage returns or line feeds. Then, use a comma as a string constant (",") to separate string expressions in the PRINT# statement. Data items will be separated on the disk by a comma and read back as different strings by INPUT#.

Using Personal Computer Software Workbook

- Suppose you have output string values loaded with commas, semicolons,
  significant leading and trailing blanks, etc. You must write them to a
  disk and surround them with explicit quotation marks, CHR$(34). Under
  these circumstances, consider using WRITE# instead.

First, let's build a file with numeric data, retrieve, and display it:

```
10 OPEN "O",1,"NUMDATA"          Opens sequential file for output.
20 A = 3 : B = 6 : C = 9
30 PRINT#1,A;B;C                 Writes numeric data to the file.
40 CLOSE 1                       Closes the file.
50 OPEN "I",1,"NUMDATA"          Opens same sequential file for input.
60 INPUT#1,X,Y,Z                 Reads the data from the file.
70 PRINT X;Y;Z                   Displays data on the screen.
80 CLOSE 1 : END                 Closes the file.
```

                        If you enter and run this program, the output is:
     3   6   9   (and the file is recorded on disk.)

Now, let's build a file with string data, retrieve, and display it:

```
10 OPEN "O",1,"STRDATA"          Opens sequential file for output.
20 A$ = "Omaha, Nebraska"
30 B$ = "  68124"
40 PRINT#1,A$;B$                 Writes string data to the file.
50 CLOSE 1                       Closes the file.
60 OPEN "I",1,"STRDATA"          Opens same sequential file for input.
70 INPUT#1,X$,Y$                 Reads the data from the file.
80 PRINT X$;Y$                   Displays the data on the screen.
90 CLOSE 1 : END                 Closes the file.
```

                        If you enter and run this program the output is:
OmahaNebraska 68124   (and the file is recorded on disk.)

Note: the comma vanished but can be preserved if statement 40 is modified
      as follows:

40 PRINT #1,CHR$(34);A$;CHR$(34);B$;CHR$(34)

                                        Now the program yields:
Omaha, Nebraska 68124

The awkwardness of writing complex strings to sequential files and retrieving
them is largely eliminated by using the WRITE# statement. If WRITE# is used,
each data item will be separated from the preceding one by a comma, and
strings will be automatically delimited by quotation marks:

WRITE #,fn,exp   where fn is the file number used when the file was opened,
                  and exp is a list of numeric, relational, logical or string
                  expressions to be written to the file. It is not required
                  to put explicit delimiters in the list of expressions in a
                  WRITE# statement.

Now let's build the same sequential data file using WRITE# instead:

```
10 OPEN "O",1,"STRDATA"          Opens the sequential file for output.
20 A$ = "Omaha, Nebraska"
30 B$ = "  68124"
40 WRITE#1,A$,B$                 Writes data to the file.
50 CLOSE 1                       Closes the file.
60 OPEN "I",1,"STRDATA"          Reopens the same file for input.
70 INPUT#1,A$,B$                 Reads the data from the file.
80 WRITE A$,B$                   Displays data on screen using WRITE.
90 PRINT A$;B$                   Displays data on screen using PRINT.
100 CLOSE 1 : END                Closes the file.
```

When this program is entered and run, the output is:

```
"Omaha, Nebraska","  68124"      (Displayed by the WRITE statement.)
Omaha, Nebraska  68124           (Displayed by the PRINT statement.)
```

Before we leave sequential files, here is an outline of the procedures needed to update a file. Sequential files can be updated, but the procedure is a bit tricky and requires that two files be manipulated. It would be a good practice exercise for you to write a sample program from these steps and keep it as a utility:

a. Open the sequential file to be updated for input.
b. Open another new sequential file for output.
c. Input a list of data and update them as necessary.
d. Output the updated data to the new file.
e. Repeat steps c and d until all the data from the old file have been read, updated and output to the new file.
f. Close both files and consider a KILL command to erase the old file if you no longer need it, thus preserving disk space.

5. Random File Record Layout

After opening a random file you have to define the record layout by a FIELD statement. FIELD organizes the random file buffer so that you can pass data from the program to disk and vice versa. The record can be divided up into any number of fields, but the total number of bytes allocated in the FIELD statement cannot exceed the record length that was specified when the file was opened. To do so would cause a "Field overflow" error.

The FIELD statement sets up the size of each field and allows string variable names to point to each field. Ordinary string variables point to an area in memory called "string space", but field variable names point to the buffer area created when the file was open. All data, both strings and numbers, must be placed into the buffer in string form. Numerics must be converted to strings using special functions (STR$ is most common), prior to their being written to disk. Field variable names must be used with care. If they are used later in the program for LET or INPUT statements, they would be redefined, and the name would no longer point to the buffer.

FIELD fn,w1 AS x1$,w2 AS x2$,...

    where fn is the file number used when the file was opened; w1, w2, etc.
are numeric expressions specifying the number of bytes to be allocated
to the fields named by the string variables x1$, x2$, etc.

10 FIELD 1,15 AS X$,10 AS Y$ allocates the first 15 positions of the
    random file buffer 1 to the string name X$
    and the next 10 to Y$.

20 FIELD 1,5 AS Z$,20 AS Q$ allocates the first five positions of the
    random file buffer 1 (same file) to the
    string name Z$ and the next 20 to Q$.

Note: You may use FIELD statements any number of times to reorganize the file
buffer. They do not cancel each other. Numerous field names can
reference the same area of the buffer. But, if two successive field
statements use the same variable name, the first will have been
redefined by the second. It is good practice that the sum of all field
widths equal the record length, but it is not mandatory.

6. Reading Random File Records

    To read records from a random file you must open it, specifying "R" as
access mode. The GET statement allows you to read a record from a random
file. When executing a GET statement, the contents of the specified record
is transferred into the file buffer:

GET fn,r   where fn is the file number specified when the file was opened
    and r is a numeric expression indicating the record number to
    be read. If r is omitted, the current record number (one
    higher than the last record accessed) is read. If the file is
    being accessed for the first time, the current record is 1.

Now, let's pull information out of a random file and display it:

```
10 OPEN "R",1,"RANFILE",30      Opens the file with a 50-byte record.
20 FIELD 1,20 AS A$,10 AS B$    Defines and labels two 25-byte fields.
20 FOR I=1 TO 2
30   GET 1,I                    Reads record I of the file.
40   PRINT A$;B$;TAB(31)I       Displays the contents of the record
50 NEXT I                       and the record number I.
60 CLOSE : END                  Closes the file.
```

    When this program is entered and run, the output is:

```
Delta Software, Inc.        1
Omaha, Nebraska    68124    2    (If that is how A$ and B$ were written.)
```

Note: If leading or trailing blanks or any delimiters of any sort are present
in the file, GET will bring them back for display. All ASCII
characters are candidates for GET.

7. Writing Records to a Random File

The PUT statement allows you to write a record to a random file and resembles the GET statement in reverse. The GET statement cannot operate without a FIELD statement, and neither can PUT. In addition, the contents of the record must be prepared within the random file buffer using either an LSET or RSET statement. Both LSET and RSET move data from memory to the buffer by allocating string expression names appearing in the FIELD statements.

If the string expression uses fewer bytes than you had allocated in the FIELD statement, the extra space is automatically padded with blanks. The blanks can be set to the left or the right of the string expression:

LSET s$=x$
RSET s$=x$ where s$ is the field name of the string variable defined in
                 the FIELD statement and c$ is a string expression for the data
                 to be placed into the field. LSET left-justifies the string in
                 the field, whereas RSET right-justifies it.

Note: Should the length of x$ exceed s$, characters are lopped off the right
      end of x$ in either LSET or RSET.

Now the data can be written to the random file:

PUT fn,r   where fn is the file number specified in the OPEN statement and
                r is a numeric expression for the record number in the file
                that will receive the data. If omitted, the current record
                number is assumed (as in GET).

```
10 OPEN "R",1,"RANFILE",30        Opens a random file with 30-byte records.
20 FIELD 1,20 AS A$,10 AS B$      Defines the fields.
30 X$="Omaha, Nebraska"
40 Y$="68124"
50 LSET A$ = X$                   Inserts the string data into the buffer.
60 LSET B$ = Y$
70 PUT 1,1                        Writes the data to the first record.
80 GET 1,1                        Retrieves the first record.
90 PRINT A$;B$                    Displays the data on the screen.
100 CLOSE : END                   Closes the file.
```

When this program is entered and run, the output is:

Omaha, Nebraska   68124   (Note how trailing blanks were padded.)

There are several BASIC expressions to convert numeric data to strings so that they can be written to a random file:

MKI$/MKS$/MKD$ where MKI$ converts an integer to a 2-character string;
                      MKS$ converts a single precision numeric to a 4-character
                      string; MKD$ converts a double precision value to an
                      8-character string.

Once the numeric data has been converted to the string and written to the
file, it can be read from the file as a string and converted back to the
numeric for further numeric operations:

CVI/CVS/CVD   where CVI converts a 2-character string to an integer; CVS
               converts a 4-character string to a single precision number; CVD
               converts an 8-character string to a double-precision number.

Both conversion processes can be illustrated:

```
10 OPEN "R",1,"RANFILE",14
20 FIELD 1,2 AS X$,4 AS Y$,8 AS Z$
30 X = 34 : Y = 1124
40 Z = X/Y
50 LSET X$ = MKI$(X)            Converts 34 to a 2-character string.
60 LSET Y$ = MKS$(Y)            Converts 1124 to a 4-character string.
70 LSET Z$ = MKD$(Z)            Converts quotient to an 8-character string.
80 PUT 1,1                      Writes data to file.
90 GET 1,1                      Retrieves the data from the file.
100 P = CVI(X$)                 Converts X$ to an integer P.
110 Q = CVS(Y$)                 Converts Y$ to single precision number Q.
120 R = CVD(Z$)                 Converts Z$ to double precision number R.
130 PRINT P;Q;R                 Displays data on screen.
140 CLOSE : END                 Closes the file.
```

When this program is entered and run, the output is:

34 1124 3.024911E-02

Now, watch what happens when we substitute STR$ for MKI$, MKS$, and MKD$; and
at the same time, substitute VAL for CVI,CVS, and CVD. The output is:

3 112   3.02491   because STR$ produces an extra leading blank which wound
                    up being written to the file. The other digits were
                    truncated.

Note: Still, STR$ and VAL could have been used to preserve all the informa-
      tion, (and without increasing the record length of the file), provided
      the RIGHT$ function is also used. Do you see how?

     Random files can be updated without building a new file if the order in
which records appear is not crucial. If order is important, however, a new
file will have to be built in a similar fashion as the procedure outlined for
sequential files. Consider writing a program to perform this utility:

     a. Open the random file and divide the buffer into fields.
     b. Read the record to be updated.
     c. Extract data from the buffer for display or assign them to program
        variables.
     d. Insert new values into the buffer fields.
     e. Write the updated record to the file. Go to b. to repeat if necessary.
     f. Close the file.

C. Graphics and Sound Using BASICA

BASIC for the PC can display any of the 255 ASCII characters, individual points (pixels), draw lines and produce a host of complex shapes. Even without a color monitor, the screen can be controlled surprisingly well to augment text and report data formally using charts, tables and so on. Color graphics are available with the right hardware (a color graphics circuit card and a color monitor), but even the monochrome display can be used to make the dullest of text and numbers seem interesting. First, let us look at what can be done with only green, amber, or white on black screens.

1. Screen and Cursor Control

As you project more and more data on a screen, it eventually gets cluttered, and you need to see things on a "clean slate." Also, once full, additional PRINT or WRITE statements are forced in at the bottom, and the top line disappears. This is more difficult to read than text display being written from the top down, the way we normally read a book or anything else. Consider using CLS to clear the entire screen and reposition the cursor at the first row and first column. CLS is particularly effective when used with INKEY$ to interrupt a looping display of information:

```
10 FOR I=1 TO 100
20   X = X + 1                    Counts the lines being printed.
30   IF X < 24 THEN 70            Checks to see if screen is full.
40   PRINT "Press any key..."     Screen is full.  Prompt in line 24.
50   Z$=INKEY$:IF Z$="" THEN 50   Waits for a keystroke.
60   CLS : X = 0                  Clears the screen and Reset line counter.
70   PRINT TAB(X+1);I,X           Prints display.
80 NEXT I
90 END
```

Actually, you can position the cursor anywhere on the screen to display data by using the LOCATE command. The screen contains 25 rows and either 80 (default) or 40 columns (if reset using WIDTH):

LOCATE r,c   where the first two parameters are required and indicate the row r and column c where you want display to start.

Note: Row 25 is available for display, but only if you issue a KEY OFF command prior to LOCATE. However, once KEY OFF is activated, CLS will also erase row 25. Issue a KEY ON to relight the standard display.

Even if you do not have a color monitor the COLOR command is useful for enhancing screen display:

COLOR f,bk,br   where f is a numeric expression (0 to 31) triggering the foreground color of the screen; bk is a numeric expression (0 to 7) triggering the background color; and br is a numeric expression triggering the color of the outside border. Both bk and br are optional.

Monochrome Colors Available in foreground:	Color/Graphics Monitor Colors Available in foreground and border:	
0 Black	0 Black	8 Gray
1 Underlined Characters	1 Blue	9 Light Blue
2-7 White/Amber/Green	2 Green	10 Light Green
	3 Cyan	11 Light Cyan
(Background or Border can be Black or White.)	4 Red	12 Light Red
	5 Magenta	13 Light Magenta
	6 Brown	14 Yellow
	7 White	15 High-Intensity White
	(Background limited to colors 0-7.)	

Setting the foreground colors equal to 16 + any number in the above table will cause the display to flash. Therefore, any foreground color number from 16 to 31 flashes whatever you display on the screen. Note that the color monitor foreground and border colors are arranged so that by adding 8 to any "regular" color produces a high-intensity version of that color. A few other characteristics of the COLOR command are worth noting:

- If the foreground color is set equal to the background color, characters lose visibility.

- The COLOR statement cannot end in a comma. Otherwise, you will receive a "Missing operand" error.

- The border screen is seldom displayed by most software, because BASICA supports it, but other BASICs do not. If you have BASICA, try it. Here is a sample program illustrating COLOR, LOCATE and CLS all at once:

```
10 CLS:KEY OFF                       Clears the screen and frees row 25.
20 A$ = " Changing Colors "
30 FOR I=0 TO 7
40    LOCATE I*2+1,I*8+2            Changes cursor position.
50    COLOR I,0,                    Changes foreground color.
60    PRINT A$;                     Displays the string as specified.
70    COLOR 0,I                     Converts to reverse image print.
80    LOCATE I*2+2,I*8+2            Positions string just below previous one.
90    PRINT A$;                     Displays the string in reverse print.
100   FOR J=1 TO 1000:NEXT J        Pause a moment between colors.
110 NEXT I
120 LOCATE 25,35                    Positions cursor in row 25, column 35.
130 COLOR 0,I-1                     Invokes reverse image printing.
140 PRINT " Press Q only to Quit...";
150 Z$=INKEY$:IF Z$="" THEN 150     Freezes execution. Awaits keystroke.
160 IF Z$ = "Q" THEN 180            If Q is pressed, program ends.
170 GOTO 10                         Repeats entire program.
180 COLOR 7,0 : END                 Returns to "standard screen" colors.
```

See if you can revise the program to flash the display as well.

There are a few more graphical tricks available even if you only have a monochrome monitor and no color graphics adapter. Quite a few interesting figures and shapes can be drawn using some of the ASCII codes and defining strings with them. First, consider displaying all the ASCII codes on the screen with a program similar to this one:

```
10 CLS:KEY OFF
20 FOR I=1 TO 255
30   PRINT TAB(Z*13)CHR$(I);I;       Prints an ASCII and its numeric identifier.
40   Z = Z + 1                       Increments a tab counter on each row.
50   IF Z = 6 THEN Z = 0 : PRINT     Resets tab counter and goes to next row.
60   IF I <> 138 THEN 110            Checks for a full screen.
70   X$=INKEY$:IF X$="" THEN 70      Pauses between screens.
80   LOCATE 25,1
90   PRINT "Press any key..."
100   CLS
110 NEXT I
```

You will note after running the above program that many of the ASCII characters are already set up for drawing lines, shading in various intensities, printing Greek letters and other international symbols. If you try to print either of the above two screens produced by the program, your printer will be unable to handle about half of them. The screen, however, can show them all, with the exception of the null string and the blank. Here is a simple program using several of the ASCIIs to draw a framed digital clock and add some shading:

```
10 T$ = STRING$(80,220)       Top of frame.
20 B$ = STRING$(80,223)       Bottom of frame.
30 S$ = CHR$(219)             Side parts of frame
40 H$ = STRING$(78,176)       Shading string.
50 CLS : KEY OFF
60 PRINT T$;                  Prints the top.
70 FOR I=1 TO 21
80   PRINT S$;H$;S$;          Prints 21 side parts and shading.
90 NEXT I
100 PRINT B$;                 Prints the bottom.
110 LOCATE 11,32              Positions cursor near center of frame.
120 PRINT DATE$,TIME$;        Prints the date and time.
130 GOTO 110                  Runs your digital clock.
```

You will have to enter Crtl Break from the keyboard to stop the clock and continue. The CHR$(177) and CHR$(178) are also available for shading using different patterns and intensities. If you are clever, you should be able to modify the above program so that as the clock runs, every 30 seconds or so the screen is reconstructed with a different shading intensity. Hint: use VAL in conjunction with the TIME$ function, and set up a new variable which is incremented periodically.

Other graphic possibilities using the ASCII codes are limited only by your imagination. The two functions that are most useful for linking up ASCII codes to form tailored graphic characters are STRING$ and CHR$. A worthwhile project would be to build a personal dictionary of individually fabricated graphics characters that you can utilize from one program to the next.

2. Drawing Figures and Painting

This section is applicable only to PCs equipped with a color graphics monitor adaptor circuit. Without this card, you will receive an "Illegal function call" message should programs shown here be run. There are several graphic statements and functions set aside in BASICA that allow you to write programs to produce versatile graphic images. The most elementary graphic function is that of plotting the position of a single point:

```
PRESET (x,y)
PSET (x,y),c    where x and y (mandatory) are coordinates on the screen for a
                point. The color c (optional for PSET) is black if set to 0
                and white if 1 (default). If PSET or PRESET is encountered, the
                pixel at coordinates x,y on the screen is illuminated.
```

Note: Two resolutions determine how many pixels are available: medium and high. In medium resolution (40 column width) your screen contains 320 horizontal points and 200 verticals. In high resolution (80 column width) your screen contains 640 horizontal points and 200 verticals. Many graphics software packages elect medium resolution to take advantage of two color palettes that are unavailable in high resolution.

The (0,0) origin is set at the home (upper left) position on the screen. Therefore, the furthest point to the lower left corner that can be accessed by PSET or PRESET is (319,199) in medium resolution and (639,199) in high. We will use high resolution to illustrate graphics. Try this program:

```
10 CLS                          Positions cursor in home position.
20 FOR I = 0 TO 639
30  FOR J = 0 TO 199
50   PSET(I,J)                   Illuminates pixel.
60  NEXT J                       Draws line vertically.
70 NEXT I                        Moves to next right pixel.
```

The above program will eventually paint the entire screen in foreground color. Enter Crtl Break if you tire of watching it. Now let's draw some boxes and let you set the starting location and size:

```
10 INPUT "Horizontal starting location (0 to 639)";X
20 INPUT "Vertical starting location (0 to 199)";Y
30 INPUT "Length of sides (0 to 199);S
40 CLS
50 FOR I = X TO X + S
60  PSET(I,Y)                    Draws top of box.
70  PSET(I,Y+S)                  Draws bottom of box.
80 NEXT I
90 FOR J = Y TO Y + S
100  PSET(X,J)                   Draws left side of box.
110  PSET (X+S,J)                Draws right side of box.
120 NEXT J
130 STOP:GOTO 10                 (enter CONT to continue...)
```

Now, see if you can add statements to connect the 4 corners with diagonals.

Engineers frequently have to draw broken lines to indicate hidden edges on a
drawing. Broken lines make solid lines appear to stand out. By adding a step
function to a loop, pixels are skipped, and broken lines are drawn:

```
10 INPUT "Vertical starting position (1 TO 199)";Y
20 INPUT "Size of step";S
30 CLS
40 FOR X = 0 TO 639 STEP S          Sets the STEP function
50   PSET(X,Y)                      Draws the broken line.
60 NEXT X
70 STOP:GOTO 10
```

If you were able to draw the diagonals for the boxes on the previous program,
see if you can convert the diagonals to broken lines.... Looping is one way
to draw lines in BASICA, but a special function is available to do it at
incredible speed:

LINE (x1,y1)-(x2,y2),c,BF

   where x1,y1 are the coordinates of the starting point of the line; x2,y2
   are the coordinates of the end point of the line, c is an optional color
   number (see PSET); B (optional) allows you to trace a rectangle whose
   diagonal is defined by (x1,y1),(x2,y2) coordinates; F (optional and
   available only if B is used) shades in the whole rectangle. IF x1,y1 is
   omitted, the starting point is the last point drawn.

LINE can be used to draw line charts, bar charts and all sorts of shapes if
curved lines are not required. Consider this program, which positions a bar
on the X-axis.

```
10 INPUT "Bar height (1 to 199)";H
20 INPUT "Bar width (5 to 300)";W
30 CLS
40 LINE (1,1)-(1,199)               Draws Y-axis.
50 LINE -(639,199)                  Draws X-axis.
60 H = 199 - H                      Sets the y2 coordinate based on H.
70 LINE (50,199)-(W+50,H),BF        Draws the bar, starting at x1 = 50.
80 STOP:GOTO 10                     Enter CONT to draw another bar.
```

     Not everything is straight, rectangular, or square. A BASICA function
has also been set aside to draw circles and ellipses. A somewhat simplified
version of the CIRCLE statement command is presented:

CIRCLE x,y,r,,,,a   where x and y are the coordinates of the center of an
                         ellipse; r = the radius of the major axis of the
                         ellipse; a = numeric expression setting the aspect of
                         the ellipse:

 - The aspect defines the ratio between the vertical and horizontal axes of an
   ellipse. If a = 5/12 in high resolution or 5/6 in medium resolution, a
   circle is drawn. The smaller the aspect is, the flatter the ellipse, the
   larger the aspect is, the taller the ellipse.

- The last point referenced when an ellipse is drawn is the center of the ellipse. Points that fall off the screen (if r is too big) are not drawn.

The following program draws an ellipse in the center of the screen and encases it in a box:

```
10 CLS
20 CIRCLE (120,100),60,,,,5/15        Draws the ellipse.
30 LINE (40,10)-(260,190)             Draws the box.
```

Shading in the figures you have drawn has already been made possible by the LINE command options. But LINE will not shade in ellipses per se. To shade them in we can use the PAINT statement:

PAINT (x,y),c,b   where x and y are the coordinates of pixel where painting begins; c is the color to be painted with (defaults to 1) and b is the boundary color (defaults to 1). In high resolution, b is meaningless.

Now, we can PAINT the ellipse we drew inside the box:

```
10 CLS
20 CIRCLE (120,100),60,,,,5/15
30 LINE (40,10)-(260,190)
40 PAINT (120,100)                    The entire ellipse is painted.
```

As an exercise, see if you can use looping to draw several ellipses and boxes all over the screen and paint the ellipses. Then, see if you can paint the boxes while leaving the ellipses alone.

3. Audio Capabilities

By now, you have already heard the PC make a sound when it boots. The speaker can be controlled in BASICA to produce sounds of all frequencies and even produce music. The simplest command to produce an audible tone is:

BEEP which is identical to the statement PRINT CHR$(7);.

BEEP is commonly used to alert users when an input error has been made while using a program. Consider incorporating BEEP into error trapping routines as an effective alarm or to notify users when the program is taking a periodic branch. However, do not overuse it. Remember the boy that cried "Wolf!" too often?

```
10 INPUT "Select your option (1 to 10);OP
20 IF OP > 0 AND OP < 11 THEN 60          Is input valid?
30 BEEP                                   Sounds alarm.
40 PRINT "*** Invalid option specified."  Notifies in writing.
50 GOTO 10                                Tries again.
60 PRINT "Option";O;"successfully selected."
70 REM program continues from here.
```

Your audio possibilities are extended remarkably in BASICA by using the SOUND statement. With it you can generate different frequencies and harness the clock running in the central processor to set the tempo and control the duration of the tones you produce:

SOUND fr,d   where fr is the frequency in Hertz of the tone, ranging from 37
                to 32767; d is the duration in clock ticks, ranging from 0 to
                65535.

- The clock ticks 18.2 times per second. Therefore, if d = 18, the duration
  of the tone is about one second.

- Periods of silence can be created using f = 32000 or so, followed by the
  required duration, as no one can hear that high; and, the speaker cannot
  produce the sound anyway.

Here is a sample musical note table with corresponding frequencies:

Note	Frequency	Note	Frequency	Note	Frequency
C	130.81	C	523.25	C	2093.00
D	146.83	D	587.33	D	2349.40
E	164.81	E	659.26	E	2637.00
F	174.61	F	698.46	F	2793.80
G	196.00	G	783.99	G	3136.00
A	220.00	A	880.00	A	3520.00
B	246.94	B	987.77	B	3951.00
C	261.63	C	1046.50	C	4186.00
D	293.66	D	1174.70	D	4698.80
E	329.63	E	1318.50	E	5274.00
F	349.23	F	1396.90	F	5587.60
G	392.00	G	1568.00	G	6272.00
A	440.00	A	1760.00	A	7040.00
B	493.88	B	1975.50	B	7902.00
B A S S		M I D R A N G E		T R E B L E	

- Middle C is at a frequency of 523.25.

- To obtain frequencies of tones lower than those shown in the bass column,
  halve the frequency of the octave just above. To obtain frequencies of
  tones higher than those shown in the treble column, double the frequency of
  the octave just below.

Tempos can be set by setting the duration between subsequent tones produced in
a loop, coupled with the pause between duration. The clock ticks 1092 times
per minute. Simply divide the number of beats per minute you desire into 1092
to obtain the required d-value for setting the duration required for each
beat. Depending on how fast you want to play your music, d will range
anywhere from about 5 to 30 for each beat. An average tempo is about 10,
because the scale is not linear.

Using Personal Computer Software Workbook

The following program can be used to test your hearing by playing continuously
higher tones in steps. The tones increase in frequency non-linearly but are
played for the same duration of about 3 seconds each:

```
10 CLS
20 LOCATE 10,10
30 PRINT "Press any key to sound a tone..."
40 Z$=INKEY$:IF Z$="" THEN 40
50 CLS
60 X = X + 1: Y = Y + 50
70 F = Y * X                          Increments the frequency.
80 IF F > 25300 THEN 130              Checks for inaudible pitch.
90 PRINT "Frequency is";F;"Hertz."    Displays frequency.
100 SOUND F,55                        Sounds the tone.
110 SOUND 32676,10                    Notifies sound is off.
120 GOTO 20
130 PRINT "End of Test."
140 END
```

The above audiologist's program can be made even more scientific if you first
compute all the frequencies and load them into an array, F(22). Then,
scramble them randomly prior to sounding them. That would eliminate order
bias during the test. The test would end after 22 different tones have been
played. Can you put it together?

And, to end this section of your workbook on a melodious note, consider
playing the five notes made famous by the visitors from outer space who
provided us all with a close encounter:

```
10 CLS
20 LOCATE 10,10
30 PRINT "Press any key to continue..."
40 Z$=INKEY$:IF Z$="" THEN 40
50 DATA 440,493.9,392,196,293.7       Frequency data.
60 READ A,B,C,LC,D                    Reads notes.
70 FOR I = 1 TO 2                     Plays tune twice.
80 SOUND A * I,18
90 SOUND B * I,18
100 SOUND C * I,18
110 SOUND LC * I,18
120 SOUND D * I,25
130 SOUND 32767,36                    Pauses between tunes.
140 NEXT I                            Jumps an octave.
150 PRINT "Press Q to stop the music."
160 PRINT "(any other key for an encore)"
170 Z$=INPUT$(1):IF Z$="Q" THEN 190
180 CLS:GOTO 70
190 END
```

Change the tempo and the octaves as you see fit, maestro.

SELF EVALUATING QUIZ

1. BASICA has three modes of operation: _____, _____, and _____.

2. A BASICA program line can range in value between _____ and _____.

3. The command used to correct program lines is the _____ command.

4. If the program you want to enter into the PC's memory is already stored on disk, two commands may be used to retrieve it: _____ or _____.

5. If you want to retain a new program on disk for future use, then you must issue a _____ command to store it on disk.

6. To erase a program or file stored on disk, a _____ command is used, but to erase individual BASIC program lines, you must issue a _____ command.

7. The _____ statement sets the upper bound on subscripts of a(n) _____ variable and allocates memory storage locations.

8. The _____ statement creates an internal data file when a BASIC program is run; the _____ statement allows the PC to access the internal file.

9. You are using the INPUT statement to read in a numeric value from the keyboard. Your friend enters "Hello." The PC responds with _____.

10. Jerry Jones wants the PC to accept entire sentences, full of punctuation, as input to his program. Jerry should use the _____ statement.

11. Ruth Wilson just picked up a listing of a BASIC program written by her friend, Sally. There are # signs appearing everywhere in clusters. Sally must be employing the _____ statement for formal output.

12. The _____ function returns the numeric value that is the ASCII code of a string constant, and the _____ function returns a one-character string corresponding to the ASCII code.

13. Jack Fletcher wants the PC to read just one value from the keyboard and move on to the next instruction in his program. Two string functions are available: the _____ and _____.

14. Harry Smith's data are strings containing city names and zip codes. Harry can display a list of the zip codes alone by using the _____, _____, or _____ functions after reading the data.

15. Objective: create a string composed of 25 consecutive dollar signs. Solution: use the _____ function and forget looping.

16. Objective: create a string constant composed of 35 blank spaces. Solution: use the _____ function, or your answer to 15 (above).

17. Sheila Sanders just completed the first entry into the PC of a large program. After seven runs, she continues to have bugs in it. Sheila should consider using the _____ and _____ statements to help end her frustration and find all the bugs.

18. The _____ statement triggers the beginning of an error handling routine, but three other functions are mandatory for it to work. They are _____, _____, and _____.

19. Judy Jackson just constructed a sequential file on disk. She has now written a program which opens the same file for Output. Therefore, Judy is in the process of _____ her file.

20. In order to add more data to the end of a sequential file, the easiest way is to write a program which opens the file in _____ mode.

21. Jack Hammer needs to access a large sequential file but display only a portion of it. Jack must first open the file in _____ mode and then use the _____ function.

22. Susan Smith's program writes a sequential file. If she intends to read data from the same file without ending her program, she must first _____ the file by issuing a _____ command.

23. If you intend to output numeric data from a sequential file, you may use either _____ or _____ to separate the expressions.

24. Quotation marks, spaces, commas, semicolons, and carriage returns are sometimes globally referred to by the term _____.

25. Harmon Kirkpatrick is preparing to build a sequential text file derived from one of his term papers. Harmon should open the file in _____ mode and write to the file using the _____ statement. Later, he can retrieve the text using the _____ statement after opening the file in _____ mode.

26. After opening a random file in _____ mode, the record _____ must be specified, and the record layout defined by a _____ statement.

27. All data, before being written to a random file must be placed into the file _____ in _____ form.

28. The contents of any specific record of a random file are transferred into the file buffer when the file is read using a _____ statement.

29. Before data can be written to a random file using a _____ statement, either _____ or _____ must be used first to move data from the PC's memory to the file buffer.

30. _____, _____, _____, or _____ are BASIC functions that convert numeric data to strings so that they can be written to a random file.

31. Numeric data stored on a random file as a string can be retrieved as a string by a _____ statement and then converted to numerics by using a _____, _____, _____ or even a _____ function.

32. Sarah Struthers has written a program that will clear the screen using a _____ statement and position the cursor for display using a _____ statement prior to a PRINT.

33. Jim Bryan wants to position the cursor on row 25 of his screen to display a prompt. Before he can do this, he must give the PC a _____ command.

34. Larry Ashford loves to highlight screen display using reverse image printing with his monochrome monitor. The statement he uses most to do this is _____ prior to a PRINT.

35. The date entered when DOS was used to boot the PC can be printed using the _____ function, whereas the time can be displayed using _____.

36. Pixels are illuminated individually in color graphics mode by using either the _____ or _____ functions in conjunction with coordinates.

37. Entire lines can be drawn or rectangles shaded in with color graphics PCs, provided you employ the _____ statement.

38. John Borden just tried to draw a Circle on his monochrome monitor using the CIRCLE statement. John's PC gave him a _____ message.

39. Mary Lamb just completed a program that plays a tune in honor of her name. Therefore, Mary has learned to use the _____ statement.

40. The clock in the PC ticks _____ times per second.

SOLUTIONS

1. Command; Execute; Edit
2. 0; 65529
3. EDIT
4. LOAD; RUN
5. SAVE
6. KILL; DELETE
7. DIM; array
8. DATA; READ
9. ?Redo from start
10. LINE INPUT
11. PRINT USING
12. ASC; CHR$
13. INKEY$; INPUT$
14. RIGHT$; MID$; VAL
15. STRING$
16. SPACE$
17. TRON; TROFF
18. ON ERROR GOTO; ERR; ERL; ERROR
19. erasing or deleting
20. Append
21. Input; LOC
22. close; CLOSE
23. commas; semicolons
24. delimiters
25. Output; WRITE#; LINE INPUT#; Input
26. "R"; length; FIELD
27. buffer; string
28. GET
29. PUT; LSET; RSET
30. MKI$; MKS$; MKD$; STR$
31. GET; CVI; CVS; CVD; VAL
32. CLS; LOCATE
33. KEY OFF
34. COLOR (0,7)
35. DATE$; TIME$
36. PSET; PRESET
37. LINE
38. Illegal function call
39. SOUND
40. 18.2

PRACTICE ASSIGNMENTS

1. Start the BASICA interpreter on the DOS disk. Type anything but a statement number, followed by return. How does the PC respond?

2. Enter a simple program to print your name and student number on the screen, and purposely make several errors. Run it. Then use the EDIT command to fix all the erroneous statements and the DELETE command to erase unnecessary lines.

3. As you read this workbook, enter every sample program into the computer as you go along. Be sure you try not to run them all in one session.

4. Save all your programs you enter as you read section 5 of this workbook on a working, formatted diskette. Use the FILES command to keep track of the directory and remaining disk space (shown on DOS 2.0 or higher).

5. Save a program by an erroneous file name on purpose; back the file up by saving it correctly. Then, erase the erroneous file. Use the FILES command to verify your results.

6. Use the DIM and DATA statements to develop an internal file of all 12 months in a calendar year. READ the months and PRINT them on the screen, together with the current year, using a loop.

7. Perform 6 (above), but instead of building an internal data file, enter all the data from the keyboard using INPUT lodged in a loop until all months are entered.

8. Keep the stub the next time you buy groceries. Use it to build an internal data file of the prices and names of items you bought. Write a program that will exactly replicate the stub on the screen or with your printer, including taxes, amount paid, and change. You will have to use PRINT USING (or LPRINT USING) if you want to do the project right.

9. See if you can do 8 (above) with a program that exactly replicates the cash register itself at the supermarket. All prices must be entered from the keyboard (try the num pad) and results displayed on the screen or printer immediately as if the register tape was running. Do not clutter the screen or the printer with extraneous characters that flaw the replication.

10. Set an error trap in your program in 9 (above) so that any price over $25 beeps the speaker and is screened from the subtotal.

11. Create a sequential file on disk that holds the first 20 names and telephone numbers in the phone book. Print the file back out and display the data exactly as it appears in the book. Then, see if you can write a program that prints the names back in reverse alphabetical order.

12. Open the file in 11 and append 10 more names to the list. Print the file again. Then try to insert a name and telephone number from another page somewhere in your file. Reprint the file to prove your success.

13. Do both 11 and 12 (above), only this time create a random file instead.

14. If you have color graphics, revise the clock program shown in this chapter so that the date and time appear inside a painted circle.

15. Compose the birthday song and print the words on the screen as it plays.